BABYSELLING

BABY SELLING

*The Scandal
of
Black-Market
Adoption
by*

NANCY C. BAKER

Foreword by
SENATOR HARRISON A. WILLIAMS, JR.

The Vanguard Press
New York

Copyright © 1978 by Nancy C. Baker
Published by Vanguard Press, Inc.,
424 Madison Avenue, New York, New York 10017.
Published simultaneously in Canada by
Gage Publishing Co., Agincourt, Ontario.
Library of Congress Catalogue Card Number: 77-93231
ISBN: 0-8149-0798-9
Designer: Tom Torre Bevans
Manufactured in the United States of America.

To my son Bradley

Author's Acknowledgments

A list of all the people who gave information and time to help me research this book would surely require another in itself. I do, however, particularly want to thank the many who spoke to me about what is, for them, a highly emotional and difficult subject—the release of a child for adoption or their search for, and adoption of, a child through the black market. Their candidness about their heartbreaking situations is most appreciated and, I hope, will help others avoid similar tragedies. As promised, the names of those whose stories are included herein have been changed.

I also received a great deal of co-operation from many members of the news media who have written about black-market adoption. Especially generous with their time and advice were: Pam Zekman of the *Chicago Sun-Times;* Lynne McTaggart of *The New York Daily News;* Fred Francis of NBC-TV NEWS in Miami; George Frank of United Press International in Sacramento; and Patt Morrison of *The Los Angeles Times.* Many thanks to all.

Two assistant district attorneys deserve particular appreciation as well. Richard Moss, of Los Angeles, and Joseph Morello, of Manhattan, have dedicated a large part of their professional efforts over the past several years to investigating and prosecuting babysellers. These two should be commended for their tenacity in pursuing some extremely difficult legal cases. Both men were most generous with their time in discussing not only their own work, but the legal aspects of black-market adoption throughout the nation as well.

My appreciation, too, to Vice President Walter Mondale and his staff. During his tenure in the Senate, Mr. Mondale worked untiringly as an advocate of children's rights, and he and his staff supplied me with a wealth of information about their investigations of black-market adoption and children in foster care.

On a more personal level, I want to thank Eric Lasher and Shelly Lowenkopf for their generous encouragement and friendship during the planning, researching, and writing of this book. My gratitude, too, to Tom Woll, who did the editing.

And last, but never least, my warm appreciation to my good friend Carol Kerner, who read every word of this book in manuscript form and contributed her most perceptive editorial advice.

—N.C.B.

CONTENTS

FOREWORD

BY

Senator Harrison A. Williams, Jr.

Few things can so deeply offend the sensibilities of Americans as the notion of treating children as commodities to be bought and sold in a black market. It is more shocking, still, that this practice is allowed to flourish in virtually every area of our nation.

In recent years, the economics of baby selling have opened avenues of trafficking which extend across state, and even national, boundaries. It is the interstate and international aspect of the problem which permits—and in my view mandates—intervention by the Federal government.

Years of careful documentation have built the case for action by lawmakers. Yet there is still no Federal law prohibiting the sale of children across state lines.

Baby black markets exist primarily for the benefit of a small number of unlicensed adoption brokers, many of whom unscrupulously exploit the emotions and uncertainties of their clients. Unwed mothers, confused and misinformed, are cajoled into giving up their newly born children for sale. The misfortunes, fears, hopes, and frustrations of couples who have been unable to adopt children through legitimate adoption agencies are played upon until the couple, in desperation, is willing to pay almost any price for aid in securing a healthy, normal child.

Yet, the greatest and most tragic victim can be the child who is sold. The broker involved in this sort of transaction is seldom concerned with the qualifications of the adopting parents. More important, the broker rarely provides a reliable and complete medical history from the mother, possibly concealing serious diseases which could cause permanent harm if not treated promptly. The motive of those involved in the black market is not humanitarian concern for the natural mother and prospective parents. The motive is one of pure personal profit.

Methods employed in baby sales follow a recurring pattern. A pregnant woman, usually an unwed teenager, is contacted by an adoption broker or referred to him by contacts in abortion clinics and private medical practices. She is offered the concealment of her pregnancy and a promise of a good home for her child. In the last three months of her pregnancy she is brought to a city on the East Coast where she is provided with food, shelter, and an allowance, often allowing her to live in a degree of luxury she has never before encountered. All expenses connected with the delivery are paid by the baby broker. After the birth a surrender agreement is signed and the child is transferred to the previously selected parents. If the mother should attempt to extricate herself from the arrangement, she is threatened with the prospect of reimbursing the broker for all the expenses incurred over the past few months. This pressure almost invariably results in the surrender of the child.

For his role in providing the prospective parents with a child, the broker receives what is referred to as a finder fee. This fee, varying in amount, has been known to range as high as $40,000. As in most commodity markets, the price is determined by the economic forces of supply and demand. I cannot imagine a clearer and more concise indictment of the immorality of the tragic practice of selling children than this. We are not just dealing with the sale of human life and the future course that life will take. We are witnessing the sale of an individual's identity. We must not allow it to continue.

The regular transporting of women and babies between states and across national boundaries makes this black market sale an interstate crime. Agencies in individual states are not capable of conducting the necessary investigations into the majority of cases involving other states and countries, It has been pointed out that in cases involving the importation of women from foreign countries to give up their babies, the State Department, Immigration Service, and others may hesitate to commit their resources because there has been no clear violation of existing Federal law. Lack of Federal action has greatly encouraged those who sell children to continue and even to expand their activities. I have introduced legislation which is intended to provide needed Federal law which is now nonexistent. The thrust of my proposal is to prohibit the adoption of any child through arrangements that have not been made through licensed agencies and individuals, but rather have been accomplished by the use of barter and coercion. The infants are defenseless in this matter which will decide the direction their lives will take and they must be protected.

As Chairman of the Senate Human Resources Committee and author of legislation in the 95th Congress to outlaw babyselling and expand opportunities for legitimate adoption, I am very grateful for Nancy Baker's timely and forthright treatment of this sensitive subject. By reviewing case after heartbreaking case of abuse and fraud in babyselling, Ms. Baker provides a warning to unwed mothers and prospective adoptive parents, while making the strongest possible justification for immediate Federal action. The author suggests that public apathy may explain why, after over a decade of Federal interest in this area, very little has been done. By shedding welcome light on the underworld of babyselling, this book may be just what we need to speed enactment of a strong Federal law banning this practice once and for all.

—H.A.W.

The Black Market in Babies

John and Mary Keller have a desire they share with most American couples. They want children.

They also have a problem. One of them is infertile.

A few years ago, the Kellers' problem could have been solved relatively easily through adoption, since there was an abundance of healthy white infants available. But, today, conditions have changed.

John and Mary called several adoption agencies in their home town and received essentially the same answer from all of them: "We just haven't any babies; plan on waiting at least five years." "We're placing only older and handicapped children, no babies." "We are no longer accepting applications for adoption."

The agencies explained that the combination of legalized abortion, changed attitudes toward unwed mothers keeping their babies, and better methods of birth control had virtually halted the supply of adoptable babies.

Ten years ago, eighty percent of unwed pregnant girls and women gave up their babies for adoption. Today, it is just the opposite—eighty percent keep their infants to raise themselves. And, of course, many sexually active unmarried girls and women are either using birth control successfully or are legally aborting their unwanted pregnancies.

As an example of how acute the baby shortage has become, the number of babies placed for adoption in 1975 by the Los Angeles County Adoption Agency (the world's largest) was only one-tenth the number it placed in 1965. At the same time, adoption officials are noting an increase in couples like the Kellers, who want to adopt.

John and Mary were terribly disappointed by the agencies' response, but they didn't give up hope altogether. They talked about their problem with friends, neighbors, doctors. Then, one day they received a phone call from an attorney they'd never met.

"I understand you want to adopt a baby," he said. "I have a girl about to deliver. Are you interested?"

To the Kellers, this call seemed to come from heaven. They had heard about independent adoption, the "gray market," but thought there were no babies there either. They were assured that this would be a legal adoption. They would undergo a home study done by a county adoption agency, though it would not be done until they already had the baby in their home. The attorney assured the Kellers that their chances of having the baby taken away because they had been found unsuitable were, under these circumstances, virtually nil. After the home study, the adoption would be approved in court. It was merely a formality to go to court at all, he told them.

There was only one hitch. "My expenses are high in this kind of thing, with the baby shortage and all," the lawyer said, "and the mother wants a little something for her trouble. Just to help her get back on her feet."

With the medical bills, attorney's fees, and the "little something" for the mother, the Kellers were told to expect to pay around six thousand dollars. The medical expenses and the one-thousand-dollar attorney's fee could be paid by check. The remainder had to be in cash.

John and Mary hesitated. Why cash? The transaction had begun to sound strange. But the attorney reassured them. He required cash because the law prohibited giving the mother more than her medical expenses. However, that presented no problem, he said, because they wouldn't be telling the court about the cash payment.

If John and Mary Keller had thought about it, they would have realized they'd have to perjure themselves when the adoption court requested a list of the expenses paid in connection with the adoption. But the Kellers didn't want to think; they wanted the baby.

They had one day to make up their minds. If the Kellers wouldn't pay, somebody else certainly would. The attorney had a long list of couples who wanted to adopt a baby like this one. The Kellers thought it over and decided to accept the attorney's reassurances about the money and his claims that the baby's natural mother was a pretty cheerleader and its natural father a married college professor. This would be a beautiful baby. And it would be theirs.

The Kellers bought nursery furniture and fixed up the baby's bedroom. They cleaned out their savings account and borrowed money from relatives. Then they awaited the birth of their baby.

It was a Thursday night when the attorney called again. The baby had been born—a healthy, seven-pound girl with a shock of blond hair. There was just one little problem. Mary and John looked at each other and their hearts almost stopped beating.

"Nothing too serious," the attorney said. "It's just that another couple wants this baby too, and they're willing to go to eight thousand dollars. Now, since I talked to you first, I'll give it to you if you'll go to, say, ten thousand." This baby sale had become an auction.

John and Mary Keller didn't get that baby. They didn't have the extra four thousand dollars. Since they were basically honest people, they couldn't go along with what had become an obviously illegal situation, either. Somebody, however, had not only the extra money but fewer scruples. Somebody bought that baby.

What happened to the Kellers is happening all over the country today. There are thousands of couples anxious to adopt a baby—an estimated two hundred hopeful couples competing for every healthy white infant available for adoption. Several thousand of these couples each year become desperate enough to pay babysellers up to fifty thousand dollars for the opportunity to become parents.

Joseph Reid, Executive Director of the Child Welfare League of America, estimates at least one-third of the independent (non-agency) adoptions—some five thousand babies this year—are black-market adoptions (transactions in which money, not the child's welfare, is the paramount factor). And, as the shortage of adoptable babies worsens, that figure will rise.

Five thousand is just a ball-park figure, Reid stresses, and may actually be low. It's hard to tell how many independent adoptions may have involved inordinate sums of money, or even how many adoptions there are of any kind nationwide. There is no legal requirement for states to report the number of adoptions within their boundaries to the federal government; while the Department of Health, Education, and Welfare attempts to collect data on adoptions, all fifty states seldom report, and what figures are available are, at best, several years out of date.

Whatever the actual number of black-market transactions per year, almost everyone knowledgeable about adoption agrees that babies have become a commodity in the United States, something sold to the highest bidder. The shortage has put infants in demand like so many sacks of coffee beans or tanks of gasoline. And, when there is a shortage of anything, by the law of supply and demand, prices climb.

Babies are human beings, however, not coffee or gasoline. Selling people was supposedly outlawed in America when slavery was abolished. So how can this be happening here? The question will be answered in this book, which will discuss why babyselling has become commonplace; why the babysellers are not particularly worried about being arrested and convicted; and why everybody involved in a black-market adoption—the natural parents, the adoptive parents, and, most of all, the baby—stands to lose. Everybody, that is, except the baby broker, who just gets richer and richer. Black-market adoption is big business. The going rate for healthy white infants has been climbing continually in the past few years, reaching a reported high of fifty thousand dollars for a "made-to-order" baby. And the end is not in sight.

There are three kinds of adoptions between non-relatives. (Many adoptions each year involve children and their stepparents or relatives within the third degree; these adoptions will not be dealt with here.) The first type is agency adoption, where all details are handled by a state-licensed adoption agency. Competency of agencies, like state licensing requirements, varies widely.

The second type is independent adoption, often called the gray market. Here, the adoption is arranged by the natural mother herself, or by a middleman, usually an attorney or physician. The fees involved generally cover medical expenses of the natural mother and a reasonable attorney's charge. (Medical expenses should be thoroughly documented and the attorney's fee should not be much more than one thousand dollars, according to most adoption experts.)

Gray-market adoptions are useful for a variety of people, including the natural mother who desires to choose a home for her baby without dealing with an agency; couples who do not meet strict agency requirements—who are, for example, older than thirty-five, of a mixed or minority religious background, or who cannot medically prove sterility. Proponents of independent adoption say it serves as a valuable alternative to an agency monopoly and prevents adoption from becoming an exclusively white, Christian-oriented service. Independent adoptions are now legal in all but four states.

The third type, and the one with which this book is most concerned, is black-market adoption. This often functions much like the gray market because it is arranged by a non-licensed intermediary who is a liaison between the natural mother and the adoptive parents, but the sky is the limit when it comes to the fee he charges. On the black market, babies are literally sold and their hereditary backgrounds are often misrepresented to bring a higher price.

The determining factor in whether an adoption should be categorized as black market is the importance of money in the transaction. The sum varies widely—from a direct sale of a child for, say, as little as five hundred dollars up to fifty thousand dollars or more. If the money that changes hands is what determines whether a certain couple gets a certain baby, it is a black-market deal no matter how much or how little is involved financially.

Black-market adoptions are riddled with fraud. The baby offered to the Kellers, reportedly the issue of a pretty cheerleader and a college professor, was more likely born of a fifteen-year-old high-school dropout and her gang-member boy friend. But if the truth were told, the child's price tag would have to be lowered. In black-market adoptions the baby's natural mother may not have wanted to give up her child. She may well have been tricked or coerced into doing so and, as a result, may later try to withdraw her consent. The natural father almost surely was never contacted for his consent at all. And chances are excellent that nearly all the money involved—including the "fat" in the medical expenses and the "little something" for the mother—ended up in the baby broker's pocket. And that broker knew nothing about the adoptive family's moral background, age, stability of marriage, religious background, or psychological health. He didn't care, as long as his price was met.

Most adoptive parents who venture, or stumble, into the black market are basically good people, though one must question their judgment when they allow themselves to take part in buying what will become their son or daughter. What will they tell that child when it grows up and asks about its origins? "We paid fifteen thousand in cash for you in a hospital parking lot?" But there are enough cases of unacceptable adoptive parents on record to give one pause: adoptive parents who bought babies and were later found to be child abusers or molesters, who had terminal illnesses at the time of the adoption, who adopted to save their foundering marriages, who were alcoholics and drug abusers.

Black-market adoption is a disgrace; an even greater disgrace is that very little is being done to stop it. Congress has been trying for more than twenty years to pass federal legislation to deal with babysellers, but there are still no federal laws. We have laws dealing with the interstate transportation of animals, but not with the interstate transportation of children for adoption. State laws on adoption vary fifty different ways. Babysellers need do little more than become involved in an interstate transaction to hog-tie law-enforcement officials at the state level. And they know this well. Often they get the adoptive parents from one state and the natural mother from another. The attorney might reside in a third state. Who has jurisdiction over the adoption? Many adoption courts don't inquire about fees paid in another state, and if they do, the adoptive parents simply lie. They have committed perjury, but their chances of being caught and prosecuted are slight.

What if the natural mother wants her baby back? To what court does she go? She usually doesn't even know in what state the people who have her baby live.

If the adoptive parents are found to be unfit, which state has jurisdiction over the baby? The one in which it was born? The one in which its natural mother lives? The one in which its adoptive parents live?

It's not hard to see why state officials have an almost impossible time enforcing what laws they do have. As a result, there have been only a handful of court cases involving babyselling and, as this is being written, only one case that resulted in a felony conviction.

This book will take a long, hard look at the black-market adoption situation in America today and at how this multimillion-dollar business is flourishing. It will look at the people involved—the natural mothers, the adoptive parents, the babies, and the baby brokers. It will look at what law enforcement officials are attempting to do about the problem and at the tools they badly need to make the eradication of babyselling possible. And, finally, it will survey the alternatives to the black market for couples who want to adopt a child legitimately.

More than one hundred years after the abolition of slavery in this country, it's about time we stopped allowing children to be bought and sold.

CHAPTER ONE

Anatomy of a
Babyselling Business

The ad read: "Don't have that abortion. Have your child and a Caribbean vacation at the same time. All expenses paid. Plus five dollars an hour for light work suitable to pregnancy. Call Save A Life Adoption Service." It featured a picture of swaying palm trees when it ran in the *Los Angeles Free Press* and included a phone number at which someone from Save A Life could be reached twenty-four hours a day.

Slightly less flamboyant ads for Save A Life, placed by a group of Californians later indicted on charges connected with babyselling, ran in the *Los Angeles Times* and the *Santa Ana Register*. Two of the group, Ronald Silverton and Wayman O. Wilkes, received the first felony convictions related to babyselling in the United States. Others indicted were Norman Minnis, a salesman; his wife, Beverly Jean Minnis; and Lee Shaykin, an attorney.

The Los Angeles District Attorney's office acted on complaints it received from various sources to put Silverton and his operation out of business before they could reach their projected potential, but evidence seized in connection with the case's prosecution can be used to estimate the scope of similar operations.

The five were indicted in connection with two separate incidents of babyselling at ten thousand dollars each: one to a New Jersey couple and one to a New York couple. Silverton and a secretary, Lucy Sam, were also indicted later in Riverside County, California, in connection with an alleged sale of a baby to undercover agents for eleven thousand dollars. That case resulted in a hung jury and the District Attorney there dismissed it because he felt the Los Angeles indictment, which posed a time conflict, was the stronger case.

Ronald Silverton is a former Los Angeles County Crime Commissioner and a disbarred attorney. He spent ten months in state prison on an insurance-fraud-conspiracy conviction. During the years he was a practicing attorney, Silverton said he handled approximately one thousand adoptions, many of which were for Jewish couples living in Mexico City, who, he said, were unable to adopt under Mexican law because they were not Catholics.

Silverton's other adoptions, most of which took place during the 1960s when babies for adoption were in plentiful supply, were to couples on the East Coast, particularly in New York City. Prices for infants were lower then, usually around three thousand dollars, but that was high for the times.

After Silverton's release from prison in early 1973, he conspired with two other convicted felons, Wayman O. Wilkes, a former chiropractor who had served time for performing an illegal abortion (ironic in light of the fact the group said a major purpose of Save A Life was to prevent abortion), and Norman Minnis, whom Silverton met during his incarceration. Together, they discovered that Silverton's old adoption game had become much more lucrative due to the baby shortage. People would pay astronomical fees for a baby—and Silverton still had all his old contacts, particularly lawyers in other states, who could supply him with names of people who wanted to adopt. The main problem was to get enough babies to meet the demand.

Had Silverton been able to reach his goals before being indicted, he would have needed plenty of babies. In one document seized by the District Attorney's office, Silverton projected that Save A Life would place, during its first year of operation, one baby per day! His financial projection was an astounding $3,372,000 cumulative net income during the first two years of operation. The prices Save A Life quoted to prospective adoptive parents ranged from ten thousand to twenty thousand dollars per baby; maintenance and medical expenses for the natural mothers were to come out of those fees. By any method of mathematics, Silverton was aiming for a high-volume business. At one point, according to Richard Moss, the Assistant District Attorney who prosecuted the case, Silverton even planned to sell stock in Save A Life for four thousand dollars a share!

Silverton and his cohorts had, throughout the United States and in foreign countries, contacts who would supply babies. "Among the states involved," Moss said, "were California, Oregon, Arizona, Utah, Arkansas, Massachusetts, New York, New Jersey, Florida, and Louisiana. Evidence obtained also indicated connections with Canada, Mexico, England, Ireland, Denmark, Yugoslavia, Spain, and a number of Caribbean islands." The court transcript also includes testimony indicating that babymaking, as well as babyselling, may have been planned and, in one case, had allegedly been carried out.

Silverton's original plan, as the advertisement stated, was apparently to transport pregnant girls to a Caribbean island, variously identified as either St. Martin or St. Charles. There the girls were to stay in a hotel and do simple work. After they had given birth, and signed away their babies, they would collect approximately three thousand dollars in "wages" and the babies would be adopted under Dutch law. Moss said his office could find no evidence that the Caribbean situation really existed, but it is unknown whether it had just not been implemented or if it was merely a ploy to entice pregnant girls.

Jackie H. answered one of the ads. "They had a deal where you fly to the Caribbean island. They have a hotel set up which is owned by them. You work there for five dollars an hour. All you do is answer phones and work around the place and you collect three thousand when you leave." She was shown the location of the hotel on a map and told she could choose the adoptive parents for her baby from a book Silverton had in his possession.

Jackie thought the "deal" sounded wonderful and agreed to travel to the island. Instead, she waited two weeks while nothing happened and was then sent to Gardon Grove, California, to stay at the home of a woman named Shirley Comeione. Ms. Comeione had housed and chaperoned unwed mothers in the past and agreed to do so for Silverton after a friend recommended her to him. (It was lucky for the girls that Ms. Comeione did become involved.) Jackie was told to be patient.

"I sat around waiting because all I got was, you know, 'We can't take you right now. You can't fly right now because we have another girl who's making up her mind.' That was the first story I got. Then another that the hotel I was supposed to go to was not ready.

"I got kind of suspicious and that's when I contacted David Leavitt to find out what was going on," Jackie said.

David Leavitt, a Beverly Hills attorney who specialized in legal matters involving children, particularly adoptions, has become a national spokesman in favor of independent adoption. Leavitt took the information about Save A Life from Jackie H. and passed it on to the District Attorney's Office of Los Angeles County.

A second girl who answered a Save A Life ad was Debbie M., who was visited at her home by Norman Minnis.

"He asked me if I liked to travel," she said, "and I told him I did. He said perhaps we would go to the Caribbean and stay in a place for unwed mothers. We'd be flown to the Caribbean as soon as they located another girl to go with me because they didn't like to send the girls alone.

"They would send a chaperone with us and we would fly there and stay in a hotel and do light work—answer telephones and such. We could stay for up to three months after we had the baby and earn up to approximately three hundred dollars a month."

Debbie, too, ended up at Shirley Comeione's house, along with Jackie. The girls began comparing notes and Ms. Comeione became suspicious of the Silverton operation. She wisely counseled the girls not to go through with the adoptions and to tell Silverton they had decided to keep their babies, then to make other adoption arrangements.

Both girls followed her advice. Debbie gave up her baby through other channels and apparently was not bothered again by Save A Life. Jackie, however, was in for more pursuit. In late November 1973, Silverton called the father of her unborn child, Tom R., with a proposition. If Tom could convince Jackie to go through with the Save A Life adoption, he was promised, among other unspecified benefits, a flight to the Caribbean island to visit her during her pregnancy.

This proposition, too, was passed on to the District Attorney's office and Jackie was asked to help collect additional evidence against Silverton and his crew. The day after the proposition was made, Jackie and Investigator Howard Wheeler, who posed as her boy friend Tom, went to Silverton's house. Jackie indicated she might be convinced to go along with the adoption, and laid down no conditions.

Wheeler later told the court, "Silverton offered to pay Jackie fifty dollars a week for what was termed "maintenance," and also offered to pay up to one thousand dollars to anybody who had given money to her in the past during her term of pregnancy.

"We discussed this . . . and other offers, such as Silverton's paying Jackie's rent in her apartment through June of 1974. . . . He made offers to pay her phone bill and offered me twenty-five dollars for every trip I had to make to transport Jackie to the doctor.

"Numerous times I advised Silverton that I had never given Jackie any money because my financial situation would not allow me to do so. I told him I was an unemployed gardener, but he requested I sign a statement saying something to the effect that he would give me twelve hundred dollars as reimbursement for monies I had already paid Jackie during her prenatal care."

When "Tom" refused to sign the paper, Silverton offered him a "good-paying job," Wheeler said.

Like Debbie M., Jackie H. also gave up her baby through other channels.

Another source of complaint against Save A Life originated with a pregnant teen-ager, a Utah girl who had also been receiving maintenance payments from Silverton.

When her father found out about the payments, he complained to the Utah authorities. They, in turn, complained to the California State Department of Health, which passed on details to the Los Angeles County District Attorney.

Though the ads for pregnant women were getting some response, Silverton and his group spread out in their efforts to find more babies for adoption. They contacted abortion clinics, medical doctors, foreign sources, and right-to-life agencies. Few stones were left unturned.

One rather amusing misunderstanding occurred with Right-to-Life Counselor Jane Pendergast when Silverton called her at the Newport Beach office where she volunteers time, to ask if she had access to the names of pregnant women who had decided against abortions.

"He told me he was from some kind of a lifeline, too," she said, "but he didn't tell me what it was. He said he wanted to help girls get their babies adopted.

"On occasion, we do meet pregnant girls and he asked me if I could refer them to him. I asked him what he did and he said he was a lawyer. He said he would be able to supply the girls with more money than they would usually get.

"I asked him, 'What kind of parent?' He said, 'Real good people. We're looking for real good babies.' And he said the parents would be willing to pay as much as five-thousand dollars for the baby.

"I was beginning to think it was odd," Mrs. Pendergast said. "At first he sounded as if he wanted to help babies." Now she was not so sure.

She told Silverton she was not interested in money, but in babies. So he changed his tactics from the usual offer of money for referrals. "He said to me, 'If you would be interested in having a baby yourself, I could get you one in thirty days if you give me the names of five girls who are pregnant,' " she said.

Mrs. Pendergast found the situation ludicrous. "I already had four children and I was having another. I didn't need a free baby."

A more typical contact was made with an investigator, Edmond Aleks, posing as Michael Colvin, a family-planning director in Bakersfield. His first discussion took place with Wayman Wilkes who offered him five hundred dollars and set up a meeting with Silverton. At the meeting Silverton told Aleks that Save a Life paid mothers who accepted its offer a certain maintenance fee and that it had attorneys working in every state of the union to refer parents. Nevertheless, the one thing Silverton desperately needed was Caucasian babies to fill the demand.

Aleks, as Colvin, was offered five hundred dollars for his first referral of a pregnant woman and one thousand for each subsequent referral. Silverton painted a rosy financial picture for the family-planning director: "He said I could, by referring babies and referring other people who would refer babies, make a hundred thousand a year," Aleks said.

Still another variation of the scheme was offered to David Hunter, owner and administrator of Altadena Community Hospital, a facility where abortions are performed. The first enticement offered was contacts. "He [Silverton] said he was an attorney and a CPA and that he had a great number of contacts with doctors," Hunter said. "He said he could possibly introduce me to these doctors so I could have business.

"But he said, 'My primary occupation is the adoption

referral business. It is perfectly legal. It's sanctioned by the Dutch government.'

"Silverton said he was looking for girls, pregnant girls —Caucasians—that he would sign to a work contract for approximately three thousand dollars. The girls would be flown to a Dutch island in the Caribbean. Then, when they had had the baby, they would be given the three thousand and a plane ticket home and he would retain the baby."

Then came a further incentive for Hunter and the specific details of what he was to do for Save A Life. "Silverton said he would make it worth my while financially if I would arrange to hire a girl and put her in the hospital dressed as a nurse. Her function would be to talk any girl there for a therapeutic abortion out of that abortion."

Planned Parenthood (PP) was another target. G. Roderick Durham, director of PP's Orange County office, was first contacted by Silverton in September, 1973.

"He said he was operating an adoption agency that was not licensed, but was legal in all fifty states, and he was looking for sources of referral for pregnant girls who were desirous of placing their children for adoption.

"He told me these children were placed out of California if their residence was in the state; that the agency took care of the girls from the time of their application to the agency . . . by paying them fifty dollars a week and living expenses, taking care of their medical bills and prenatal and postnatal care; and that any referral agency such as our own would be rewarded with a fee of about one thousand dollars for making the referral." During the two months Durham was in sporadic contact with Silverton, the financial offers fluctuated from one thousand dollars to five hundred. Other offers were made. "For example, Silverton proposed to provide a full-time psychiatric counselor if we preferred that to cash."

At a meeting in November of that year, Durham asked Silverton about the cost to adoptive parents. "He replied that the adoptive parents paid the girl's costs, plus the attorney's fees, which he said were twenty-five hundred dollars. And in response to a question as to what the total fee to the adoptive parents might be, he said it ran from seventy-five hundred to ten thousand dollars."

Durham thought this very high and asked Silverton what his own profit was. "He said it was purely altruistic as far as he was concerned; that the costs of the service to the girl—her living expenses, medical care, attorney's fees, and the amount paid to the finding agency—consumed a major part of the fee and that his office received only enough to cover its expenses."

Durham reported these contacts to the regional director of Planned Parenthood and was instructed to have nothing further to do with Silverton and his organization. No referrals were made from that agency.

Other methods of finding babies were even more crude. At one time, a college student was hired to canvas campuses for women who were visibly pregnant and offer them a deal to give up their babies.

Assistant D.A. Moss described one bizarre foreign connection uncovered during a legal search of Silverton's house, where authorities found a carbon copy of a letter Silverton later denied was ever sent. Moss points out, however, that the original of the letter was not found in Silverton's files, only the carbon.

The letter, dated January 13, 1973, was to a Miss Fatima Demirovski in Belgrade, Yugoslavia. It briefly explained that Silverton had an "adoption agency" and that there was a shortage of babies in the United States. "I immediately need ten pregnant girls," it said. "After while [*sic*] I will need about one pregnant girl a week."

The letter went on:

> Immediately upon a girl becoming pregnant I shall give her two thousand new dinars (if she is already pregnant then she will immediately be eligible for the two thousand new dinars). When she becomes six months pregnant I shall trans-port [sic] her to either the United States or some other country (where my adopting clients live); there she will have the baby. I shall pay for all her living expenses from the time she comes to the country to have the baby until three months after she has the baby; this includes her medical expense of having the baby. After she has the baby and she consents to an adoption by my clients I shall give her an airplane ticket back to her home in Yugoslavia and twenty-four thousand new dinars.
>
> In return for your help I shall give you one thousand new dinars for each girl who becomes pregnant or is already pregnant who permits us to transport her to the country for the adoption.

It was signed by Ronald R. Silverton.

Especially significant is the phrase, "Immediately upon a girl becoming pregnant . . ." which implies that Save A Life was interested not only in performing a service for unwed mothers but in creating new lives as well. In fact, here a financial incentive was being offered to entice women to *become* pregnant for the sole purpose of having their babies adopted.

Additionally, this letter indicates that a woman would have little chance of changing her mind about the adoption after giving birth: she would be stranded in a foreign country, since the ticket home would not be forthcoming until "after she has the baby and she consents to an adoption by my clients."

Richard Moss said evidence of a British connection—Josephine Flynn—was found in Silverton's effects as well. Apparently he had approached Ms. Flynn with much the same deal he offered Fatima Demirovski. (Josephine Flynn achieved additional notoriety in early 1976 when, according to the *London Sunday Mirror*, she "was sentenced in London to six months' imprisonment, suspended for two years, for controlling prostitutes in the Mayfair Escort Service.")

Another revealing document seized on the Silverton search warrant was a promotional leaflet intended to help sell stock in Save A Life Adoption Service. Entitled, "Son or Daughter," it read:

> Facilitating the independent adoption by a qualified couple of an infant boy or girl is the service to be provided.
>
> Client couples will initially come from a list of approximately two hundred couples who have previously retained the law firm of Silverton Law Corporation for such facilitation. The Silverton Law Firm has been dissolved and the list is now the property of the writer.
>
> The infants will come from ladies who, in their

sixth month of pregnancy, will be entitled to live at a home provided by Son or Daughter until three months after they have had the child. When they leave they will be given one thousand dollars to aid them in their readjustment. During their stay at the home the maintenance, including good medical services, will be provided free.

Since each of the ladies will have come from another country they will receive free transportation when they arrive and when they leave. Some may desire to stay and to give birth to another child; if so they will obtain free maintenance at the home for another year, and fifteen hundred dollars when they leave.

The country in which Son or Daughter is located shall provide a court adoption within two days from the approval of both the natural mother and the adopting parents. A fee of one hundred and fifty dollars will be paid to the court for the adoption certificate.

It is conservatively anticipated that within the initial year Son or Daughter will facilitate one adoption per day.

The leaflet carried the name and address of Ronald Silverton. Moss said Silverton admitted writing the document, but claimed that "only a few" were ever distributed. Again significant is the phrase, "Some may desire to stay and to give birth to another child. . . ." More indication of intended babymaking.

Perhaps the most bizarre and distasteful episode of the Silverton operation is an incident of actual babymaking, though both Silverton and the woman involved deny it.

A search warrant was obtained for Silverton's house and office on February 6, 1974. Among the papers seized in the search was a note dated February 4, which read: "Rose Marie is fertile 8th, 9th, 10th and 11th."

"Another piece of paper, a legal pad," Richard Moss states, "was also dated 2–4–74. It read, 'Told Mrs. Castaneda H is father of baby delivered down there.'" Moss explained that capital H is lawyers' shorthand for the word husband.

"Now, Silverton said the note read, '*His* father,' not 'H is father,'" Moss said. Silverton, once an attorney himself, denied knowing about the shorthand use of H for husband.

"Bear in mind that the paper has the same date as the note about Rose Marie," Moss went on. "There was a woman by the name of Rose Marie H. [last name withheld by author] who went to a legitimate doctor on the fourth of February. Documents from the doctor's office said that the patient was referred by Mr. Ron Silverton. It listed a spouse and a home address in Rosemead. When Rose Marie testified in court, she said she was not married at that time, she wasn't living with a husband, and that she both had and had not a boy friend.

"But the home address she gave was the home of Dr. Wayman O. Wilkes," Moss said. Evidently Rose Marie was living with Dr. Wilkes and his wife as their house guest during this period.

"Among the treatment charts was a note that the doctor had removed her IUD because the patient wanted it out so she could get pregnant," Moss said. "Also seized in the search warrant was a cassette taken from Silverton's answerphone. On that, a woman's voice stated, 'Just went to see Dr. X. He says I'm fertile on the eighth of the month.

That means I can get pregnant on the eighth, ninth, tenth, and eleventh. Get somebody for me. I want to do it this month.' "

Moss said Rose Marie H. acknowledged in court that the recording was of her voice. She also claimed she "got lost" during those fertile days and woke up later, unable to recall anything that had happened to her.

Rose Marie did in fact get pregnant. She had a baby nine months and two days later and put it up for adoption with the County of Los Angeles. During her pregnancy, both Silverton and Wilkes had been indicted, so any proposed deal with her fell through.

"Rose Marie denied she had actually been paid or had been promised money for getting pregnant," Moss said. "You can draw your own conclusions—which I did in my closing statement."

Additional evidence collected indicated that the price for Rose Marie's baby was to have been twenty thousand dollars, twice what Silverton was charging for other babies at the time. Moss speculated that the Mrs. Castaneda mentioned in the note was a Mexican national and that her husband was probably the father of Rose Marie's baby.

In an interesting sidelight on the trial, Silverton denied that the Rose Marie note was in his handwriting, though a graphologist testified that, in his opinion, he definitely had written it. Silverton then brought in his own expert, a man named Henry Silver, to testify he had *not* written the note. (Silver, also a graphologist, was identified as "a quack" in a 1963 *Saturday Evening Post* article about him. He subsequently sued the *Post* for libel and lost.)

Babysellers find their customers through a loosely connected series of lawyers and doctors, usually in other states, or by word of mouth among couples seeking adoptions. Save A Life was no exception.

One potential customer served to add fuel to the prosecution's case, however. Rodney D., a Los Angeles stockbroker who looks a good ten years younger than the thirty-four he claims, ran across Silverton's name in a typical way.

Rodney and his wife had talked with friends and acquaintances about their desire to adopt a child and their lack of success with either agencies or private attorneys. During a trip to New York City, Rodney mentioned his plight to a friend, who revealed that he had adopted a child several years before and was now looking for a second. The friend had an attorney's business card sent to him by his doctor.

"This card was for a fellow living in California who said he could deliver or get children through independent adoption sources." Rodney agreed to call this "attorney"— Ronald Silverton—on his own behalf as well as his friend's when he returned to Los Angeles.

"Before I called Silverton," Rodney said, "I talked with my wife again and she said, 'Let's keep trying; let's try anything we can.'

"I called Silverton and he outlined over the phone the financial aspects of what he was doing. He mentioned a ten-thousand dollar figure. He said, 'It's going to be a cash deal, there's no receipts.' Now, as a businessman, I saw this as a blind alley. I felt it was extremely dangerous, like taking a bag of money to a blackmailer and hoping you're going to get something in return. Unless you've got marked bills, you don't have any receipt.

"So, being somewhat unsophisticated in the sense of police work, but on the other hand somewhat sophisticated in the sense of knowing what is good business and what isn't, I started to pull back. But my wife didn't want to miss an opportunity."

Rodney continued to pursue the Silverton deal, but in a more cursory way. "I played it down to a point where I told him I didn't have the capital at the moment but would later, when properties I owned were to close, and so on. I wanted to structure a situation where I wouldn't lose the contact, but at the same time could continue to learn more about it so I had a better feeling for it."

Rodney and his wife had also contacted several attorneys and had their names placed on waiting lists. At about this time, one of the attorneys, David Leavitt, called them and said he might have a baby for them soon. "I happened to mention to David the fact that I had talked with this other man and he said, 'Oh, my God! Be very careful, this man's been in jail,' and so on. I don't think he was being deleterious to the guy, but to the risks involved. At that point, David told me Silverton was being pursued by the D.A.'s office and asked if he could refer the investigators to me. I said fine, and they did later contact me."

The District Attorney's investigators had Rodney call Silverton while they taped the conversation. "They had me effectively confirm things like price, how the adoption was to be handled, and so on," he said.

Rodney became a witness for the prosecution. He and his wife later adopted two babies and, when I talked to him, were employing a pregnant Mexican maid who, ironically, was under the mistaken impression that they intended to adopt her unborn baby too. The D.s were in the process of explaining to her that their family was already complete.

One man who went through with a transaction for a child with Silverton and Save A Life also testified, though unwillingly. Dr. G., a New York pediatrician, was granted immunity from prosecution in return for his testimony. The price for his first adopted child had been three thousand dollars. Now the G.s wanted a second child. They contacted their attorney.

In October 1973, Dr. G. received a call from Silverton. "He said to me, 'Your name has been given me by your attorney and I want to put you on the adoption list. You must have only two things: you must be ready to come out here right away, and you must have payment of ten thousand in cash.' " Dr. G. told him he didn't have that kind of money at the time but asked if he could still be put on Silverton's list. The latter told him that when he had the money he should contact his attorney.

The G.s saved the ten thousand dollars and contacted their lawyer. Shortly afterward, Silverton called them again, saying he had a child, and instructed the doctor to bring the cash to California.

"Silverton met me at the airport and took me to a motel," Dr. G. related. "He showed me a picture of the mother and her parents. He said, 'Have you got the ten thousand in cash?' I gave him the money."

When Dr. G. asked why the payment was so high, Silverton told him that he had a lot of overhead, and went into the problem of how he had a lot of girls who wanted to place children but that he didn't accept everyone. A lot of the girls were drug addicts or something like that. So, in order for him to travel all around and meet the women he had to charge a large fee.

"When I was first told to bring the ten thousand in cash, I thought it a little strange. I called my attorney and he told me it was perfectly legal."

After the exchange of money, Silverton took Dr. G.

to the hospital to see the baby. Dr. G. examined the infant girl himself and found her healthy.

Dr. G. has no regret about the transaction, except having to testify at the Silverton trial. He summed up his attitude, "I would have taken a baby from Mars if they had one available."

The infant adopted by the G.s came to Silverton through the loose network of connections and word of mouth. It was born to a North Hollywood teen-ager whose mother had heard of Silverton from friends in both Colorado and Texas. The mother called him and the adoption was arranged. The cost to Silverton was a total of seven hundred and fifty dollars for the girl's doctor and hospital bills.

The history of the Save A Life prosecutions is complicated. The Los Angeles County Grand Jury filed fourteen counts against the five defendants. The thrust of the trial was to determine whether or not the babies were being sold. Assistant D.A. Moss said Silverton conceded he had received money, but "characterized his fee as a referral fee, or finder's fee, not a sales price. The contention of the prosecution was that the fee was for the sale of the child."

California statutes do not specify babyselling, so Moss had to use an old slavery statute to prosecute the case. "We used a broad statute which, in effect, says that if you receive money or anything of value in consideration of placing or causing to be placed a person under the power or control of another, you have violated the statute. That was originally envisioned as a slavery statute and that is the only penal tool that specifically met our problem," he said.

Norman and Beverly Jean Minnis were convicted of advertising an unlicensed home-finding agency. Lee Shaykin was convicted of making an unauthorized placement for adoption. They received fines for their misdemeanor convictions and Ms. Shaykin was also disciplined by the California State Bar Association.

Wayman O. Wilkes pleaded guilty to conspiracy—a felony—and was sentenced to nine months in jail. After having served most of his sentence, however, Wilkes decided to appeal his conviction.

Silverton was the only one of the five to have a jury trial. He was found guilty of operating and advertising an unlicensed home-finding agency—both misdemeanors—but was found innocent on two other misdemeanor counts. The jury failed to reach a verdict on ten additional counts and a mistrial was declared. The retrial was set for June 1975. At that point a disposition was reached. Silverton agreed to have a court trial (heard by a judge) on one felony charge of conspiracy to violate the adoption laws. By agreement, only the one charge was submitted to the judge. Nothing else.

The judge (Superior Judge Thomas T. Johnson), was the same man who had presided over the original trial. "The case was submitted to him on the basis of the first trial transcript," Moss explained, "instead of bringing in all the witnesses again. The judge could read and consider and recall the entire trial. On the basis of that, he found Silverton guilty of the felony conspiracy charge. Nothing else was submitted for determination, so there was never any finding of guilt or innocence on anything else."

Judge Johnson sentenced Silverton to six months in county jail on one misdemeanor from the original trial and added five months on the second. He placed him on probation for three years on the felony conviction from the second trial on condition that he serve the eleven months and obey all laws in the future.

Silverton appealed his conviction and, in the summer

of 1977, the California Appellate Court overturned one of the misdemeanor convictions and the felony conviction against him. The state legislature had been in the process of changing the statute relating to operating an unlicensed homefinding agency during the period the Save-A-Life infractions took place. Because of this fluke of timing, the Court said, no conviction under the old statute was legal. In the wake of the Appellate Court's decision, new charges of felony conspiracy to make an illegal placement were filed against Silverton, stemming from the same series of events. He pleaded no contest to these charges on November 29, 1977, and, at this writing, is awaiting sentencing.

Moss expressed some regret that the use of the slavery statute was not put to the full test. It was used in relation to one of the charges that stands dismissed as long as the three convictions remain valid.

Even though the outcome of People of the State of California *v.* Ronald Silverton *et al.* might not have been as severe a setback for babysellers as some might have hoped, it did prove that prosecutions are possible. In order to prosecute, however, both a district attorney who acknowledges the scope of the problem, and a great deal of money for investigative staff time are needed. Luckily, Los Angeles County had both.

Given even those two factors, however, Richard Moss probably would not have pursued the case had Silverton still been a practicing attorney. "It's hard to prosecute lawyers because they have this umbrella that they're functioning as a lawyer and processing an adoption for a fee." Since there is no law stating that a thousand-dollar attorney's fee for handling an adoption is legitimate while a ten-thousand-dollar fee is not, on what basis could an indictment be obtained?

Another problem Moss and his investigators faced also occurs in other states. If California is the home of the natural mother, she (and her parents, if she is a minor) must sign papers in court releasing the child for adoption. If the adopting parents live in another state, that state ends up with these papers. So, after the fact, there is no permanent record in California of who adopted this child. A record of the infant's birth remains, but not of his adoption. In addition, adoption records are sealed by law and courts vary in their willingness to order the records unsealed to aid babyseller prosecutions. Moss was fortunate that the California Superior Court was completely cooperative, for that is not always the norm. The vital records on a child born in California may well be sealed if that child is sold to parents residing in a less cooperative state.

The expense and time involved in prosecuting the Save A Life Adoption Service were worthwhile, Richard Moss feels. It put the organization out of business, but, perhaps even more important, it also seems to have curtailed babyselling in California.

"I had several attorneys call me after Silverton was indicted to ask my advice about whether or not they should get into the business themselves," Moss said. These attorneys seemed most interested in whether or not Silverton was likely to get a felony conviction. If he had received only a misdemeanor conviction, some would have perceived that legal risk as simply part of the cost of doing a lucrative business.

It is to be hoped, too, that the Silverton case may have set a precedent for the prosecution of babysellers elsewhere, since it did result in the first felony conviction of a babyseller in the United States. Given the proper laws and the proper people enforcing them, baby brokers can be put out of business.

CHAPTER TWO

The Baby Buyers—
Adoptive Parents

The people who pay outrageous amounts of money to adopt a baby come from all kinds of life styles and from all parts of the country. The majority are probably good parents—some definitely are not.

The baby buyers have their differences, but they also have things in common: the prospective fathers are often professionals or successful businessmen. They have to be to afford fifteen or twenty thousand dollars without too much strain. Others, however, arrange second mortgages on their homes and borrow from relatives. Those persons, virtually excluded from adopting in the black market, are the lower-middle and lower classes. For them, the going rates are impossible.

A prime similarity among baby buyers is an obsession to adopt a baby. People don't risk a perjury conviction and their life savings unless they want something very much. These couples, too, want that baby badly enough to ignore any misgivings they may have about the legality and morality of black-market methods. They don't worry about what they will tell the child when he asks where he came from; they don't worry about whether the baby's natural mother was tricked or coerced into giving him up for adoption; they don't worry about whether or not this baby was the result of a pregnancy for profit, or if the mother sold her child. All these couples worry about is where to get the large sum of money this baby will cost and whether or not the courts will find out the circumstances under which the child was purchased and, possibly, take the baby away from them.

Another trait baby buyers have in common is their fear of being exposed—to the courts they suspect may take away their baby or even convict them of perjury; to their neighbors and friends who may think less of them should the adoption's details be revealed; and, ultimately, to the child itself.

For this reason, it is difficult to convince people who have bought babies to talk about their experience. The authorities face the same problem when trying to convince adoptive parents to testify against the babyselling lawyers and doctors: even when complete immunity from prosecution is guaranteed, most buyers won't talk.

One woman, who agreed to purchase a baby for ten thousand dollars—and ultimately paid a much higher amount —agreed to talk only under the cloak of anonymity.

The woman, whom I will call Cynthia Gerber, is a New Jersey librarian, married to an engineer. The Gerbers live in a comfortable suburban house and, with their combined incomes, were fortunately able to afford the approximately fifteen thousand dollars their second child eventually cost them. Their story illustrates how badly someone can want a child and the lengths to which otherwise honest people will go to get one.

The Gerbers (who now have two adopted children, both well treated and loved) are among those good parents who adopt through the black market. They feel they were victims of the baby shortage. Had there been an abundance of babies available at adoption agencies, as there had been when they adopted their first child, they would have been given a second without any problem. But they weren't so lucky.

"We have a six-year-old that we adopted from Spence-Chapin, a New York agency, very old, very reputable," Mrs. Gerber explained. "We applied for two children originally. I was an only child and felt strongly about not raising an only child. So we applied for two and they said, 'Certainly, no problem.' "

The Gerbers passed Spence–Chapin's inspection, known as one of the toughest adoption investigations in the country. There were no skeletons in the Gerbers' closet and they adopted their tiny, blond daughter, Sally, in 1971.

"We waited about a year and then went back for a second child. They told us there was no chance. It was the year the abortion law came into being, I think. That wiped them out—that and the fact that many girls were now keeping their babies.

"The agency called in all the parents who had applied for second children and said, 'We're terribly sorry; we will have to send you elsewhere.' But they had nowhere else to send us. We were to forget about second children."

Spence-Chapin, like most adoption agencies in the 1970s, changed its thrust from handling adoptions of healthy white infants to placing the so-called hard-to-place children —mentally and physically handicapped and older children. The Gerbers were told that waiting lists for healthy non-white infants were also years long.

"We wrote to every agency we could think of," Mrs. Gerber went on, "including one in Colombia. . . . We wrote to Canada, too, to every agency people mentioned. Either they didn't reply or they were terribly sorry, but they had no more children."

Desperate to the point of being obsessed with the desire to adopt a second child, the Gerbers were prime candidates for a black-market adoption. "We found the name of a New York lawyer in an article in *The New York Times*," Mrs. Gerber said. "He was called the 'dean of private adoption' and we thought, 'Ah ha, that's the thing, private adoption.' We went to see him and he said, 'I'm not sure whether or not I can help you. I'll put your names down on my list.' We had paid him a consultation fee—for his saying he didn't know if he could help us or not! He said the adoption would be expensive, about seven thousand dollars, plus attorney's fees."

The Gerbers asked the attorney why the fee was so large and were given an answer they felt they could accept: "The lawyer said the girls were kept in the best hotels, given the best of care, and so forth. It seemed reasonable to us."

Many things about the black-market adoption racket begin to sound reasonable if you become desperate enough. The Gerbers felt this was their last chance.

"One night," Mrs. Gerber said, "we got a call from an attorney in Los Angeles, who said he'd gotten our name from the New York attorney. He asked if we were still interested in adopting a baby. We said we were and he told us he had a newborn baby boy available."

The Los Angeles man described their future son to the Gerbers. When Mrs. Gerber finally saw the baby, the description didn't match. "He told us the baby was blond and blue-eyed when he was really dark. I don't know if he'd ever really seen it or not," she said.

At this point, the price went up to ten thousand dollars—in cash. The Gerbers didn't consider backing away; they'd already accepted the idea the cost would be seven thousand dollars and they could afford the extra three thousand.

"This Los Angeles lawyer was in a roaring hurry, wanted me to hop on the next plane and come out," Mrs. Gerber recalled. "There was an airline strike at the time and only one seat available in two days. It got rather hairy. We just had to calm him down and say, 'Well, we'll get there when we can and we'll take a look at the baby.' There was no commitment on either side then."

In fact, however, when Mrs. Gerber arrived in Los Angeles, the contact there took her to a bank before he took her to the hospital. At the bank she cashed a check and handed over ten thousand dollars in small bills. Then she was taken to see the baby she supposedly was under no obligation to accept. She had two doctors examine the baby, then called her husband for a go-ahead and took her newly purchased son back to New Jersey.

When asked why she thought the money had to be in cash if this were a legitimate and legal adoption, Mrs. Gerber replied nervously "There was a reason we paid him in cash. It certainly did sound odd at first, but one of the people involved told us it had to do with alimony, that the lawyer had a lot of children, some by his first wife, some by a second, and that he was supporting the first wife and those children. So we thought he wanted to keep this income hidden from his first wife." She paused and thought. "I guess we didn't really analyze the reason."

The Gerbers filed for adoption in New York State, even though they lived in New Jersey, because the New York lawyer had set up the adoption—he wanted to collect his own substantial fee for representing the Gerbers in the New

York courts. They went along with it, listing Mr. Gerber's mother's address in New York as their home.

The couple was startled when the whole deal suddenly appeared likely to fall through before the adoption became final. They received a call from an assistant district attorney in Los Angeles who was planning to prosecute the California babyseller (who turned out not to be a lawyer at all). The authorities wanted Mrs. Gerber to testify against the man who sold her her son.

In return for immunity against prosecution for her part in the transaction, Mrs. Gerber agreed to testify. The adoption was refiled in New Jersey with still another attorney and they had to process all the papers again.

"We completely resubmitted our application to the natural mother," she said. "We went back to her and said, 'Look, in view of all these circumstances and changed conditions, do you still feel the same way? Do you still want the child placed with us?' " The Gerbers had had their son for an entire year at this point, and if the natural mother had wanted him back, it would have been like giving up their own flesh and blood. "We prayed constantly for a couple of weeks until we got her answer," Mrs. Gerber said. "Fortunately, she agreed to give up the child and the adoption in New Jersey went through."

The Gerbers explained their entire experience to the New Jersey court to assure there wouldn't be a chance of something overturning the adoption at a later date. They supplied the judge with the details of all the money they paid as well as newspaper clippings about the Los Angeles babyseller, who by that time had been indicted. When they appeared before the New Jersey court, the judge's only comment was, "That was quite an ordeal you had, wasn't it?" They uncrossed their fingers, this time for good.

The adoption is now valid in New Jersey and the days of tension and fear are over for the Gerbers. They have their son legally, but it cost them two years of trauma and guilt, to say nothing of about fifteen thousand dollars. And someday they will have to explain to that child the circumstances surrounding his adoption.

The Gerbers were told at the beginning that their adoption would be expensive. If they'd been more knowledgeable, they would have known it was a black-market transaction just from the prices being quoted.

The Pattersons, a Philadelphia couple with less money, were not as lucky. They entered into what seemed to be a completely legitimate independent adoption. Then things gradually began to change.

Phyllis Patterson is a tiny woman in her mid-thirties. She survived a bout with cancer several years ago. "When I had waited five years after my cancer operation, and there was no recurrence, my doctor assured me I was cured," she said. "So I thought it would be all right for us to go ahead and adopt a baby. We'd wanted one all along, but I was afraid, with the cancer and all. . . ." Her voice trailed off as she recalled the years of anxiety she'd lived through.

The Pattersons (their name has been changed), first went to adoption agencies. "I guess I was dumb to tell them about the cancer, but I thought I should be honest. I told them I'd had it, but that I was cured."

The first agency turned them down flat. "We just can't take the chance with a cancer patient," the Pattersons were told. "You're too high a risk."

They tried three more agencies and were given the same verdict. No babies for cancer patients, cured or not.

"I was starting to worry again about the cancer, to

have my old nightmares," Phyllis Patterson said. "I began to wonder if they knew something I didn't." The couple gave up on agencies and found a lawyer who said he had a baby due in a few months that would be right for them. His fee, he said, would be twelve hundred dollars, an amount slightly on the high side for independent adoptions at that time, but not out of line. The Pattersons planned the baby's room and told friends and relatives about their impending new arrival.

A month or so later the attorney called them again and said the fee was going up a bit. "He told us the Bar Association insisted he charge two thousand dollars. We didn't know anything about the law, so we believed him. It wasn't all that much more, so we said, 'Okay, go ahead; we're still interested.' "

Once the lawyer realized that the Pattersons were willing to pay an increased fee, he called more often. They suspected he had learned of Phyllis's former illness and what that meant for them at the adoption agencies. In one call, the attorney claimed the natural mother's medical fees were going to be higher than he had estimated. "How much higher?" the Pattersons asked. "About three thousand," the lawyer said. The total amount was now over five thousand dollars, but they were afraid to back out. More than ever they believed if they didn't get this baby they would never get one.

By the time the baby was born and the Pattersons had picked it up at the hospital, the fee was more than six thousand dollars. They were reassured by their attorney that there would be no additional charges. Consider their surprise, then, when the adoption went through the court about six months later, and he sent them a bill for "court costs" of nearly a thousand dollars.

But the Pattersons didn't complain. By then they were too frightened that something would go wrong and they would lose the child. Furthermore, in order to file a complaint with the authorities, they would have to admit to perjuring themselves in court when they swore they'd paid only fifteen hundred dollars in connection with the adoption.

"We didn't go into this to *buy* a baby," Phyllis Patterson insists. "The way the fees kept rising, it was almost a painless process. It crept up on us. Then we finally realized where we were, but we didn't want to call it all off and never have a baby of our own."

The Pattersons borrowed money from relatives, friends, and a bank to pay the attorney who supplied their baby. They're still paying off the loans and will be for the next several years. There is no question of a second adoption for the Pattersons, middle-class people who had already weathered the financial crisis of cancer. There's also no possibility, for some years, of many things they'd like to give their adopted daughter—a house in the suburbs, nursery school, pretty clothes, and the toys she sees on television.

There simply isn't any money left.

Most adoptive parents are basically good people who, primarily for reasons connected to the baby shortage, become victims of the baby marketeers. There are, however, also some who not only want a baby quickly but would never qualify through an agency.

A major problem with almost all independent adoptions—both gray and black market—is that no one investigates the suitability of the home until the family has the child in its custody. Then the investigation, usually done by a public social agency, is superficial at best. The courts will rarely remove a baby from its adoptive home and order it placed elsewhere, so what incentive is there for a social worker to go into the kind of detail that would be required in a pre-placement home study?

Betty Massey, a Sacramento, California, social worker who counsels unwed mothers considering placing their children for adoption, told me of a case that illustrates the epitome of this attitude.

The social worker assigned to this case did a thorough study of the "potential" adoptive parents and found they were totally unsuitable. They had abused their adopted baby to the point of breaking its bones.

"The social worker went into court with a police report on these people and verification that they were child abusers," Ms. Massey said. "The judge still refused to remove the baby from that home. He went ahead and completed the adoption."

She feels the courts have the wrong idea about what is good for a child. They will accept almost any defect in the adoptive family rather than move the child to another home. According to Ms. Massey, this is false logic. A six-month-old baby would be much better off with a change of families than a sentence to live its life with abusive adoptive parents.

A similar case was documented in Portland, Oregon, where adoptive parents of a young girl were, years later, found to be psychotic. This surely would have been detected had a thorough pre-placement home study been conducted by a responsible social agency. Because the child was already in the home, however, the study had been cursory and it was six years later before the parents' mental problems were uncovered.

There was another case in a southern state a few years ago in which a couple whose natural children had been legally removed from their parental care because of neglect and abuse later adopted through the black market. They, of course, proceeded to abuse their new baby.

Another, more recent, case revealed that an adoptive father had a history of child-molestation convictions.

Horror stories such as these come to light only rarely, but one wonders how many adoptions are completed for families who are, at best, marginal. On the average they may not be any worse than are couples who have their own biological children, but it does seem that in cases in which a couple is given another's child to raise, that couple should meet certain minimum qualifications, most of which have nothing to do with their financial status. Society owes it to any child whose natural parents cannot keep it to place it in the best available home. With the abundance of people today who want to adopt, there is no excuse for allowing any child to be adopted by incompetent parents.

Sharon Horner of Philadelphia's Adoptive Parents Group, sums up the scrutiny of potential adoptive parents in the black market: "In the black market, I have never heard of a lawyer who did anything other than quote a fee and tell you where you can pick up the baby—usually a parking lot somewhere outside a hospital. It's cash on the line—because it's under the table—and they don't care who you are, what you are, what you want the kid for. Nothing."

CHAPTER THREE

The Baby Suppliers—
Natural Mothers

Girls and women whose babies are adopted through the black market have some harrowing stories to tell. Most of these girls bear no resemblance to the profile baby brokers give to potential adoptive parents, whether that of pretty cheerleaders or greedy young girls who want money in return for their infants.

In fact, though no one has solid statistics, most girls seem to be quite young, often only thirteen or fourteen years old, confused and victimized. They usually don't have abortions, either because they don't believe in them or, more often, because they are afraid to tell anyone they are pregnant until it is too late.

According to the National Institute of Health, about one million teen-age girls will become pregnant this year. Of that figure, 150,000 will have miscarriages, 250,000 will have abortions, and the remaining 600,000 will give birth. Of those who give birth, at least one-third will be unmarried. Most of these, in today's social climate, will keep their babies and (at times tragically) try to raise them. Some will supply the baby black market.

Brokers prey on these young girls, pregnant, alone, and frightened. The girls are usually in a depressed state, both economically and psychologically. Thus, when a broker offers them free rent and food during their pregnancy, perhaps even maternity clothes, pays their medical bills or merely instructs the girls about getting welfare money for medical bills, they are highly receptive and grateful. The most unfortunate part about a girl's accepting this kind of aid from a doctor, lawyer, or other baby broker during her pregnancy is that she then feels obligated to give up her infant even if she later decides it is a wrong decision.

In many cases, brokers have the pregnant girl sign papers—long before she delivers the child—agreeing to give up the baby in exchange for support money. The paper is legally worthless, but how many sixteen-year-olds realize that? They think they will be threatened with a lawsuit should they decide to keep their babies, and, knowing they can never repay the money given them, go along.

Girls who become involved with black-market baby brokers invariably receive no counseling. As a result, days, months, even years later, such a girl may regret her decision to have her baby adopted and seek its return. A resolution made under duress is not necessarily a good or lasting one.

Sometimes monetary pressure isn't necessary to convince a girl to give up her baby. Influence and continual harassment may be enough.

The story of Cathy, a Sacramento, California, college student, is a case in point. The main difference between Cathy and other girls in her situation is that she was somewhat more educated and knowledgeable of her rights than most. She ultimately decided to exercise those rights, but not until she had endured months of tension and heartache.

Cathy is a pretty nineteen-year-old blonde who had a good part-time job until her pregnancy forced her to quit. She decided to complete her pregnancy rather than have an abortion.

"I considered an abortion," she said, "but I just couldn't do it. For some reason—I don't know why—I couldn't do it. I thought it would be the best thing, really, but I couldn't."

By the time she decided to have her baby and had sought medical care, Cathy was six months pregnant. In order to qualify for Medi-Cal payments, she had to have a pregnancy test.

Cathy went to a local clinic for the test and an examination. "The nurse checked me and I asked her if a doctor would see me. She said, 'No,' and I felt he didn't want to have anything to do with me. Then the nurse started asking me questions; was I married and so forth. I told her I wasn't and that I was thinking about adopting out my baby.

"As soon as I mentioned that, she left the room. When she came back, she said the doctor would see me."

The doctor Cathy saw was a psychologist, not an obstetrician. "I went into his office and he told me he had these friends who were terrific people and who wanted to adopt because they couldn't have children. They didn't want to go through an agency because the wait was too long and they were getting older." Cathy later learned that the husband was twenty-nine, the wife twenty-eight.

"Then this doctor started asking me personal questions about myself and the baby's father, about our backgrounds. I gave him information I shouldn't have. I know that now, but at the time. . . ." Like most people, when the doctor began to ask questions, Cathy answered.

At that point she didn't know much about adoption. She was "just toying with the idea" as one option open to her.

But the doctor began trying to influence her. "He was telling me how groovy independent adoption was and how I could pick the parents. . . . He said agencies are terrible because you just don't have any rights; you don't know where the baby is going. If I gave the baby to an agency, he told me, it'd be in a foster home up to a year. He was really scaring me."

Cathy told the doctor she didn't know what she wanted to do. He began a campaign to influence her. "The doctor kept calling me," she said. "He'd call at seven o'clock in the morning and at ten o'clock at night to pressure me. He'd say, 'We've got to know by the end of this week, because you can't keep these people hanging.' I didn't know what to say. I didn't want to hurt anybody, but I didn't want to say yes and I didn't want to say no. I felt horrible."

About this time, Cathy decided to consider other methods of adoption. She contacted the county adoption agency and was assigned a social worker.

"Finally I told my social worker this doctor was bugging me," Cathy said, "and she called his supervisor." The next day Cathy received no call from the doctor, but she did receive one from a lawyer. Forbidden to harass the girl himself, the doctor had passed the project on to an attorney.

"The lawyer called and said she would like to meet me," Cathy said. "I thought there was no harm in that, that talking to a lawyer might be useful. So my mom and I went to see her." The attorney read them information from several typed sheets about the couple who wanted to adopt Cathy's baby.

"I got real upset at the meeting," Cathy said. "I just

didn't want to think about it. I was putting myself in a position to face something I didn't want to face."

Cathy's first impression, though, was that the lawyer was kind and had her interests at heart. "She said if I needed anything, to just call, that I shouldn't worry about anything." There was, at that time, no further description of what "anything" might include. Cathy assumed it included money, but she never asked for any.

Cathy's state of mind in the later stages of her pregnancy was typical of many unwed mothers-to-be: she was confused and depressed; she felt everyone was trying to influence her in one direction or another and she had no idea what her own desires were; she felt pressure to give up her baby for adoption not only from the lawyer, but from her social worker as well. "Not that she was really pressuring me," Cathy said, "just that she came to see me every week. Just because she was there." Cathy felt as if everyone wanted her baby.

"I had stopped toying with the idea of keeping the child because I thought it was out of the question. I had made up my mind to give the baby up. Then, toward the end of my pregnancy, I realized I'd better do something quick," Cathy said. "I had to make a decision and these people started sounding better and better to me. So I called the lawyer to tell her I had decided to let her clients be the parents."

The attorney then sent Cathy a letter confirming their telephone conversation. In the letter, she included the name and address of the prospective adoptive parents. When she read it, Cathy fell apart.

"I had told this lawyer I didn't want to know their names," she said. "It was hard enough on me and I just couldn't bear to know who they were and where they lived. I was really upset. I started to think how they would be in the same town and I'd know where they were and it was just too hard. I called the lawyer back and told her how upset I was."

The lawyer told Cathy it was a legal requirement that she know the identity of the adoptive parents in an independent adoption. Cathy decided that since she already knew who they were, she might as well go all out and meet them. She felt she might be better able to accept the adoption if she were confident the parents were good people. The attorney arranged a meeting, but Cathy went into labor the day before it was scheduled.

The meeting was rescheduled for Cathy's hospital room. She had hoped to meet the parents alone, but the attorney came with them. "She made it very uncomfortable for me; I didn't get a chance to talk to the people at all," Cathy said.

She was honest with them, telling them she thought she wanted to give up her baby daughter but was not certain. She legally had six months before she had to sign final adoption papers and she intended to use that time to make up her mind. In the meantime, she signed a hospital release form which permitted the adoptive parents to take the new baby home.

Cathy's story has a happy ending for her, but an unhappy one for the couple who wanted to adopt her baby. She decided three-and-a-half months after giving birth to keep her baby. The lawyer originally involved, and another who was a relative of the adoptive parents, exerted enormous pressure on Cathy in an effort to change her mind. Unlike most young girls in her situation, however, Cathy got some good legal advice of her own and knew her rights.

When she called the couple's lawyer to say she wanted her child back, "she just blew up at me," Cathy said. "She told me, 'I'm going to harass you whether you like it or not. Do you know what you're doing to these people?' I said, 'Look what it's doing to me. It's not like they didn't know there was a chance I'd want the baby back. Of course I don't want to hurt them, but somebody's got to be hurt.'

"The lawyer told me to get counseling. I said I'd seen just about everybody I could think of, that it was not a hasty decision."

In fact, Cathy had seen a psychiatrist for herself and had also consulted a child psychiatrist to determine whether she would be harming her baby by taking it into a new home at three months of age.

It was a wrenching experience for everybody involved. Cathy called the adoptive mother and tried to explain her position. "She was really nervous and told me, 'If you do this to us, you might just as well shoot us both.' I said, 'I can understand your hurt because I've been hurting for months and months as you are now. Try to understand me, please, and it will help.' "

The lawyer and adoptive parents tried offering Cathy money; they tried contacting the baby's natural father; they tried scaring her by saying it would mentally scar the baby for life. Cathy didn't change her mind. Finally she went to the couple's home and demanded her baby back. She was within her legal rights and they gave her the child.

Everything is now working out well for Cathy and her daughter. Cathy has gone back to work. She has no regrets about keeping her baby, but often thinks about the ordeal. "What scares me," she said, "is that this doctor is still working out of that clinic. He's around a lot of other girls in situations similar to mine. It really frightens me that some other girl is going to have to go through the same horrible experience."

It was horrible, too, for the couple who almost adopted Cathy's baby. And it was probably pretty horrible for the doctor and lawyer who couldn't deliver the merchandise. They missed out on some sizable fees.

Although Cathy's experience ended positively, most do not. She was the exception, not the rule. While Cathy was educated and cognizant of her rights, Isabel wasn't as lucky. Her story, much more commonplace than Cathy's, began in Guatemala City. Isabel worked long, hard hours in a bakery to help feed her sizable family. It was Christmas time, so there was extra work and it was late when she left the bakery one night. She was exhausted—too exhausted to outrun the four men who dragged her into a car and raped her.

Isabel was nineteen when she found out she was pregnant as a result of the rape. "I did not want to embarrass my family—my mother is very strict. So I came here to find work before my baby was born," she said in her native Spanish. "Here" is Los Angeles; Isabel is an illegal alien.

She found more than work in Los Angeles. Her job was with a middle-class family in Tarzana, a section of the city in the San Fernando Valley. The family seemed unduly interested in the fact that Isabel was pregnant and unmarried. Her work was not hard, not work at all by Isabel's standards.

"I went to work for this woman who seemed happy that I was pregnant. She kept asking if I wanted to give up my baby and I said I didn't know. She said her family had taken care of many young girls like me, and they had all been happy to give up their children."

Isabel, lost and alone in a strange country, was constantly afraid the immigration authorities would find her and deport her before her baby could be born. She listened politely to her employer, but never agreed to give up her infant.

When Isabel went into labor, she was taken to a private hospital instead of the public facility whose fees she could afford to pay. In the delirium of birth pains, she was told to sign what she thought were temporary-care papers for the baby. She signed.

It was three weeks later when she left the hospital. She does not know why she was kept so long. By then she knew she wanted to raise her child herself; she didn't want to have it adopted. She had not been permitted to see it in the hospital, though, and by now it was already living with its adoptive parents.

She contacted the lawyer who had told her to sign the papers in the hospital and told him she wanted her baby back. "The adoptive parents bought me clothes and took me to movies," she said, "their lawyer said he could fix my [citizenship] papers if I made the adoption final. They told me if I'd give up my child, there would be a lot of money waiting for me."

Isabel found out where her child was and went to see its adoptive mother. She took her baby back and brought it to a friend's house, where she was then living.

Soon the anonymous phone calls began. "They told me, 'Children have accidents very easily. Something could happen,' " she said.

Isabel thought it over. Finally she said, "I would rather that my baby be safe somewhere else than be in danger with me. So I signed their papers."

That decision bothered her though, and Isabel ultimately decided to risk deportation by starting legal proceedings to have the child returned to her. She contacted the Long Beach Legal Aid Society where attorney Carmen Ramirez was assigned to the case.

At this point, Ms. Ramirez explained, the court was interested only in the validity of the papers Isabel had signed. Since she had signed final release papers in the office of the County Adoptions Department the question for the court was: Did the Department of Adoptions exert undue pressure on Isabel?

"My client claimed that she signed the papers, but didn't understand the legal consequences," Ms. Ramirez said, "because she didn't speak English and the translator for the Adoptions Department explained the procedure to her in such a way that she could believe this was only the first part of the adoption and she would later have a chance to go to court and change her mind."

But the papers Isabel had signed were, unfortunately, final and binding. In order to have them overturned, her attorney would have to prove she signed under duress. "I was not able to prove that," Ms. Ramirez said. "Conversations between Isabel and the attorney and other people were just between her and them and I had no cooperation from them. They denied everything."

Isabel thinks she fell into a black-market baby ring. Ms. Ramirez said she suspects the attorney involved has done this kind of thing before, but has no way of proving it. "The hard thing is that adoption files are confidential and I just didn't get any cooperation from the Department of Adoptions because they felt, I think, that their reputation was on the line. They were approving the adoption."

The attorney, Ms. Ramirez said, "had an outstanding bill of two thousand dollars and I don't think that's complete. I think that's just what was on his ledger."

In addition to determining whether or not Isabel was coerced into signing the adoption papers, the judge was interested in selecting the best home for the baby. "The couple has a lot of money," Ms. Ramirez said, "and my client is employed as a domestic. The judge can take into consideration the economic status of the adoptive parents as opposed to the natural parent and say, 'Well, in view of this, I don't think the child should be returned because it's going to be living with a person who's basically a maid.' "

Another problem with this case, Ms. Ramirez felt, was the fact that Isabel did not speak English. "When you have somebody translating on the stand, you lose a lot of the punch, especially when the translator is a man. No matter what was said it just didn't carry the emotional weight of Isabel's own words."

In the end, the court did not believe Isabel's testimony. She did not get her baby back. Since her court appearance she has moved, leaving no forwarding address since she still fears the immigration authorities.

"It's just a very tragic situation," Carmen Ramirez said, her voice heavy with emotion. "I think I would not do it over again unless I was positive I could win in court. It just caused a tremendous amount of heartache."

Under the circumstances, one wonders if Isabel was sorry she had pursued the court suit. Was she in worse emotional shape now than if she had not tried to get her child returned?

"I don't know," Ms. Ramirez said, "but I sure am."

Sacramento social worker Betty Massey thinks those who give up their babies under pressure are most likely to seek the child's return later on. The agency counsels the girls, helping them explore all the options available. If a girl decides to give up her baby after such counseling, she is usually content with her decision. Ms. Massey finds that the girls she counsels are receiving a lot of fairly subtle pressure from local doctors and lawyers who favor independent adoptions.

"For example," she said, "we have one girl who went through the agency and was planning to give up her baby. Then she went to her doctor (a general practitioner) and told him. He said, 'Don't do that. I have this couple I know personally that I would like to give the baby to.' She said she preferred the county agency so a family wouldn't have to pay so much to adopt the baby and he told her, 'Well, you know, you're not going to save the family any money by going through the agency because I'm going to charge them only a five-hundred dollar adoption fee.'

"Now, he is her personal physician, but he referred her to an obstetrician for delivery, so that five hundred is strictly a finder's fee because he's not even going to deliver the baby. In my estimation, that's illegal. He told her, 'Don't tell the adoption agency. Tell them you're going to keep it.'

"I think he's really ordering her to do things differently from the way she had planned. He's applying pressure. At this point I think that girl is seriously considering going with the doctor. By doing so she gets the approval of the doctor," Ms. Massey said. "This man is going to continue to be her physician. A doctor is the one who helps you get well; he's an authority figure; he helps you when you're in pain. When a girl is lying flat on her back and the doctor is saying, 'I've got the nicest family and I'll take this baby off your hands,' he becomes her rescuer. Even during the obstetric examination he can make it hurt less. Now, that's a very subtle kind of pressure."

Ms. Massey is also upset with doctors who violate

their patients' confidence. "Some of these doctors pass a pregnant girl's name, address, and telephone number all over town," she said. "They give it to adoption lawyers and to their other patients. Then these people start contacting the girl." For someone trying to keep her condition secret, this can be devastating.

Ms. Massey was, at that time, counseling three pregnant girls, aged fifteen, seventeen, and eighteen. One of them told about an approach made to her by the nurse in a local doctor's office. "The nurse approaches the girls," Ms. Massey said, "but only if they appear to be from the middle or upper-middle class with good backgrounds.

"The nurse's pitch is familiar: This couple had been promised a child and spent a lot of time and money preparing a nursery. The girl who had promised her infant to the couple then changed her mind and decided to keep it. We had another one set up, but the wrong doctor delivered it, and no one asked the girl for the baby, so that fell through too. Now this family has had two girls who didn't give them their babies and they're really hurting. It would be so nice if you gave them your child. They have their nursery ready and everything.'

"This kind of thing feeds a girl's feeling of guilt. It creates a desire in her to rescue this family from their childlessness."

As Betty Massey documents, often the incentive for a pregnant girl to go to a baby broker is not money but a desire to please someone who charms the girl, influences her, who seems to take an interest in her. The most successful baby brokers go to great lengths to flatter the girls, to pay attention to them. Many are terribly lonely and confused and someone who seems to care can influence them greatly.

Robert Burns, a Miami attorney who has placed dozens of babies for adoption and who, at one time, ran a dormitory for pregnant girls, prides himself on the amount of attention he lavishes on the girls who come to him.

His business has been cut down recently by new Florida legislation (see p. 69 for a discussion of the changes this has brought about in that state), but Burns still handles independent adoptions on a limited level within the state.

In 1975, when Burns was operating at full speed, a reporter interviewed two of his charges, fourteen-year-old Kay and nineteen-year-old Karen. Both were living in a house provided by Burns.

Kay told her mother about her pregnancy when she was four months along. The mother had heard of Burns, signed the proper release forms for a minor, and sent Kay to Miami where she was to give birth to her baby. [The baby was later adopted by a New Jersey couple for about $8500.] Kay felt she had only two other—undesirable—options: keeping her baby, or going to a home for unwed mothers. She rejected both.

"If you were pregnant, fourteen, and had no way of supporting the baby, what would you do?" she asked. "I just got too much life ahead of me to be tied down with a kid. Just think, when I'd be twenty, the kid would be starting school. No way."

She also rejected the home for unwed mothers because she thinks they are institutions, penitentiaries for the promiscuous.

Karen was sent to Burns by her doctor in her home state of Michigan. She had tried earlier to get birth-control pills from the same doctor but, when he insisted on getting her parents' approval before prescribing them, Karen declined. While on the plane to Florida, Karen met another girl from the same home town, also destined for Burns's home, sent by the same doctor.

Karen's baby went to a Florida couple for a fee substantially less than what Kay's baby brought. Part of the reason for the lower fee was the fact that Karen did not come to Miami until she was seven months pregnant. Her maintenance costs, thus, were lower than Kay's.

When Burns was running his home for pregnant girls—what some reporters and the police called a "baby farm"—he gave each girl about thirty dollars a week for food in addition to her room and medical care. Maternity clothes were also provided. But perhaps what counted most with the girls was not the money spent on them, but the time. Burns feels no guilt about his role: "I give them the most friendship I can. I counsel them about sex. I don't want them to screw up their heads. I tell them that sex is a wonderful thing."

He later said that he spends up to fifty or sixty hours counseling each of the girls he cares for. He is proud of his business and thinks he is performing a much-needed service.

Many of his girls would agree.

Another attorney known for his personal attention to unwed mothers-to-be is New Yorker Stanley Michelman. Unlike Burns, however, Michelman couples his personal interest with a "legal contract" he asks the girls to sign agreeing to give up their babies when they are born. (Occasionally one of Burns's girls decides to keep her baby and, he says, he makes no attempt to change her mind.)

The women and girls who have dealt with Michelman all attest to his charm and the attention he lavishes on them. They like him. And that counts when a girl is in trouble and alone.

Michelman, who claims he got out of the adoption

business in late 1976, had a referral network that functioned across the United States. He would hear of pregnant girls mainly through abortion services, but he also had a system for bringing in pregnant women from European countries.

Chicago Sun-Times reporter Pam Zekman posed as a pregnant ice skater, Patricia O'Malley, and met Michelman in a Chicago hotel room. She had been referred to him by the American Women's Center after answering a newspaper ad for abortion counseling.

When she met Michelman he had brought along two Chicago girls who told Ms. Zekman they had had babies for Michelman in New York the previous fall.

"There's so much to do you just can't do it all," Cindy told her enthusiastically. Cindy said she had lived on Sixty-second Street, not far from Times Square. "We had a fabulous time. I want to go back." Ms. Zekman reported that Cindy had also been pleased with her financial arrangement with Michelman, which provided for an allowance and food.

Before she met Michelman, however, Ms. Zekman, as Patricia O'Malley, was told by Bob Schell, a counselor at the American Women's Center, to sign papers agreeing to an adoption. She described the experience:

"Schell entered the room with a form for me to sign. It was on the letterhead of Michelman & Michelman. I read the two pages of legal jargon and gradually realized I was being asked to sign a statement promising that if I did not turn over the child in my womb, I would repay every cent spent on me.

"Even though I was not pregnant—or perhaps because I was not—I hesitated. What could they do to me if I failed to turn over my firstborn? But I signed. Later, lawyers whom I consulted laughed at such a document, telling me it was nothing more than a meaningless device designed to scare the gullible into staying in line.

"Then another counselor took my picture so that the prospective parents would know what kind of baby to expect. Somehow, I felt like a breeding animal that had just been sized up, bought, and catalogued."

Papers like the ones Ms. Zekman signed do their intended job, though. Most women who sign them do believe they have to repay the money spent on them if they decide to keep their babies—and they simply do not have the money. They give up the babies.

Once her papers were signed, though, and Michelman felt "Ms. O'Malley" would, in fact, give him her baby, he became most solicitous.

Ms. Zekman wrote:

"Stanley Michelman worked hard to put me at ease. He always sounded cheerful, genuinely concerned about me . . . and able to solve all my problems.

"He said he had four apartments available in New York, including 'a fantastic place, . . . a two-bedroom luxury apartment on the East Side of Manhattan.' He said I could come any time, as long as I gave him a little notice so he could arrange for me to stay with a suitable roommate."

This kind of attention and apparent concern can mean a lot to a girl who is really in the kind of trouble Ms. Zekman was merely acting out.

One reason girls and women decide on adoption as the best course is that they think their baby will have a chance at a better life than they could offer it in a single-parent home. Additionally, they want to think that the situation has been settled satisfactorily; that the baby has the best possible parents; and that they themselves can now go on with their own lives, perhaps never able to forget about the baby they bore, but able to get on with living.

In most cases, they never hear anything further about their children.

Connie, a teen-ager from Dayton, Ohio, wasn't so lucky. She waited until it was too late to have an abortion. Friends put her in touch with a Brooklyn, New York, attorney who promised to meet her expenses and find good parents for her baby.

He told her "that the child would get a really good education, be able to go to college and, you know, have everything," Connie recalled. "And then he made the reservations for me to fly to New York."

Connie stayed, for a week, in a house in the Bronx before she gave birth to a baby boy. It was only then that she met the attorney face to face for the first time.

"He described the procedure," she said. "When I left the hospital, I would take the baby down—I had to do it, it was the law that I take the baby downstairs—and give it to him and he would give it to the people." Connie was in another room when the attorney handed her baby over to the adoptive parents. She never saw them.

Connie's baby was kept in the nursery throughout her hospital stay, and when she carried him downstairs, he was completely covered by a blanket, so she never really saw him either.

Connie's mother came to New York to co-sign adoption surrender papers that the attorney notarized and a judge of the Family Court witnessed. Connie and her mother went back to Ohio and they agreed between themselves not to mention the baby again. The adoption, they felt, gave it a chance for a much better life than they could provide.

Nine months later, though, a registered letter arrived from the attorney. In part, it read: "I've been informed that 'boy' [Connie's last name] has been brain-damaged since birth and that his condition has only been discovered recently. My clients have abandoned all intention of adoption and custody after learning about his illness. The child is presently in New York Hospital in New York City. You have the right to reclaim the child. Please communicate with me immediately."

Connie's mother described it as "the most horrifying letter I've ever gotten in my life.

"It was like they were talking about a piece of damaged merchandise, not a human being; that we had given them some damaged goods and they wanted us to come and pick them up. We had no previous warning there was anything wrong until we received the letter. When Connie read that letter, she became completely hysterical."

The closed chapter in Connie's life was suddenly wide open. "The first thing I thought," Connie recalled, "was that we should go and get him and bring him back to Dayton to take care of him. But at that point I felt helpless to do anything. I wasn't financially capable of taking care of him and I guess every mother feels a little guilt of 'What did I really do? What went wrong?' I thought maybe if I had kept him he might have been normal. I didn't know what to do. I wanted to help him."

Connie and her mother were doubly shocked because they had asked the attorney about just such a contingency before Connie went to New York to have the baby. He had assured them they were not to worry about it, that it was the problem of the adoptive parents, and that they would take care of it. "Those were his exact words, 'It would be their problem,' " Connie remembers.

Connie did not take her baby back because she decided there was no way she could care for him. He is now a ward of New York City. Something Connie had hoped she could forget has instead become a nightmare.

While most natural mothers who supply the baby black market are victims rather than profiteers, a few are not.

Robert Burns knows of a handful of women in Miami who cunningly profit from their pregnancies.

The easiest way to do this is to collect maintenance payments from several attorneys at the same time. "I've had it happen a few times where a girl is getting weekly maintenance from me, which is allowable," Burns said. "I give her the necessities of life until the baby is born. Then the girl says, 'Well, I've changed my mind.'

"In one case I found out a girl was collecting maintenance from an attorney downstairs, from another attorney around the corner, and from still a third attorney . . . and then when the baby was born, she would sell it to the highest bidder."

Most of the girls Burns deals with do not play this game. "It's a small percentage, but I know two girls who make a living that way, by having a baby a year. They've had seven or eight. I can only speculate on what happens to the baby, but I know they have one every year.

"I know this one girl ripped me off and then came back again. I said, 'Hey, you've got a poor memory. You were here last year,' to which she replied, 'Oh, that baby died.' I told her that I knew for sure that the baby didn't die and that she gave it up for adoption. I also told her I knew the three other attorneys who were paying her maintenance at the same time I was. She jumped up and ran out of my office."

Burns recently had a situation pending with one of the three girls he was currently maintaining.

"One of the girls says to me that she's been told if she goes to another attorney—I won't mention his name—she can get three thousand dollars," Burns said. "I told her, 'Look, you can do what you want. It's against the law. You're subjecting yourself to possible incarceration, jail, plus. Is that the type of fellow you want to place your child?' But, you know, a lot of these girls don't care about the children."

One woman who obviously didn't care about her children was interviewed by UPI reporters recently. The woman, Marcia, is a thirty-five-year-old street-tough New Yorker who has sold three babies.

"I sold them for the money and because I didn't want to take care of them," she said. "I'm probably not the kind of person people think of when they think of a mother.

"The first baby I decided to put up for adoption was twelve years ago. I'd been married and divorced once and was living with Bobby, a drug addict. I was keeping him supplied. I'd had two other children before that, by my first husband, but the courts took one away and the other one was taken by my father's business partner's family.

"This time I went to a lawyer in Brooklyn. I told him I was pregnant and that I wanted to put the baby up for adoption. The lawyer, who's now retired, said it would be stupid to give it to an agency, that he knew some people who would take it and would also pay me some money for it. I needed the money, so I said okay.

"I went to Pelham Bay General Hospital and my costs were paid. I think the lawyer told the people who were taking the baby how much the costs were and they paid them. I saw the people the day I left the hospital. They seemed like nice people. He's an attorney for New York City. The next week I went into court and the judge asked me if there was any objection to the adoption. I signed a paper saying there wasn't. The next day, the lawyer gave me four hundred dollars. The medical costs were over two thousand, so I had gotten about twenty-eight hundred altogether.

"Now, I don't know how much the people gave the lawyer for finding them a baby, but I know damn well it was more than four hundred."

A year later, Marcia was pregnant again. "The same people got the second kid, but it was handled by another lawyer," she said. "This time, the lawyer only gave me two hundred dollars. I was gonna complain, but he said not to mention getting any money. He said they could put me in jail if I mentioned it." (New York permits private adoptions outside licensed agencies, but prohibits payments to the natural mother beyond the normal maternity expenses incurred.)

Asked by a reporter about the payment, the attorney said it was "merely a loan." Marcia has not paid it back.

Six years ago, Marcia became pregnant again. She went to a third lawyer and offered to sell her baby.

"The next day he called and said he had someone in mind. I was almost ready to have the baby at this point, so I went to Elmhurst General Hospital and because I said I had no money and it's a city hospital, they didn't charge me anything," she said.

"So I had the baby, walked out of the hospital with it, gave it to the lawyer, and he took it across the street to this couple waiting in a car."

Marcia regrets giving up that child so easily. "The lawyer only gave me one hundred dollars after that, and even though I didn't let him know how much I wanted, I had expected more than that."

At the time she was interviewed, Marcia thought she was pregnant again.

"If I am," she said, "I'm gonna sell it. But this time I'm gonna demand at least seventy bucks a week for the time I'm pregnant and a thousand after the baby's born. I know how much a baby is worth these days. I could just let the word out that I'm willing to sell a baby and I'd have people beating my door down. After all, the lawyer is making more money than that out of this."

Marcia subsequently confirmed her pregnancy but, because of her age, decided not to risk giving birth and had an abortion. She says she doesn't know how much the attorneys made from the three babies she did sell. She doesn't particularly care. "I'm looking out for myself," she said. "The rest of the world can go to hell."

Including the children?

"Including them. I don't want to get too close to a baby emotionally, especially if I'm gonna sell it. You know, when a baby holds his arms out to you and feeds from you, you can get attached to him."

Some of the women who supply the baby market are prostitutes, and baby brokers in many areas of the country vigorously attempt to recruit them for babymaking.

For example, Nevada brothel owner Joe Conforte says two Oklahoma attorneys approached him and offered to pay up to ten thousand dollars each for babies born to his prostitutes. He says, however, that, because of the pill and easy abortions, pregnancies among the thirty to thirty-five women who work at his Reno brothel are "nonexistent."

With the high stakes involved, however, it is not hard to see why certain women would consider bearing a child for profit an alternative to the hard work of prostitution.

Several sources say there are attorneys in the eastern states who show prospective adoptive parents photographs of men and women and tell them that, for a very high price, they may select the mother and father of the baby they will adopt nine months later.

And *Philadelphia* magazine told of a woman in that city who has had two babies in the past two years. What she has to show for it is one hundred thousand dollars in cash in a safe-deposit box. She works through a New York lawyer and, for fifty thousand dollars, will fly anywhere in the country to be artificially inseminated.

It remains true, however, that most natural mothers—like Cathy, Isabel, Connie—are just naive, frightened, and confused young girls. They usually have no idea that the people who adopt their babies are paying huge sums of money to their attorneys or doctors.

These girls are still the best source of supply for the babysellers for two reasons: first, they are far more plentiful than are willing babymakers; and second, and more important, they are cheaper. It stands to reason, after all, that if a babyseller has to deal with a woman who wants top dollar for the child in her womb, there will be less money left for him.

In one way or another, most of the natural mothers in the baby black market are its victims.

CHAPTER FOUR

The Baby Brokers

The adoption entrepreneurs profiled in the following pages are not necessarily those most guilty of baby-selling. They are merely among the best known. They have made their names available to numerous couples seeking adoptions and, as a result, the news media have exposed their operations—sometimes increasing not only their notoriety but their business as well.

These baby brokers are, if anything, typical of the dozens and dozens of lesser-known men and women to be found in virtually any large city in this country. If a couple wants to buy a baby today and is willing to pay the going rates, somebody will manage to sell them one—no matter where they live.

ROBERT BURNS

"I'm not going to try to justify a ten-thousand or fifteen-thousand-dollar fee on an adoption," Robert Burns said, "but if it is wrong, then somebody who charges that fee for a criminal case is equally wrong."

Maybe Burns, the Miami-based adoption attorney,

says he can't use that kind of logic to justify legal fees in five figures, but he has used it many times to justify fees of four and five thousand in his own business. Those amounts, coupled with medical and maintenance costs for the natural mothers, have brought the total cost of a Burns adoption to eight or ten thousand dollars for many couples.

"They say, with an adoption, you're dealing with a human being, you're dealing with a life," Burns went on. "But some attorneys say, 'Give me all your money, your car, the teeth out of your mouth, and your eyeballs and I'll defend you.' They take everything a person owns, saying, 'Your freedom's at stake and I'm the only person who can help.' But that's all right. The Bar Association, the State's Attorney, say, 'That's fine.' Now, to me, that's more horrible than what they're claiming under adoptions."

One thing Robert Burns has always been, in the hundreds of adoptions he claims to have handled, is forthright. Couples who have dealt with him say they knew in advance what the adoption would cost. There might have been a slight variation if medical costs rose, but ball-park figures seldom changed significantly.

Perhaps the most unusual thing about Burns is his openness with the press. "I'm willing to talk with the press because I'm in favor of adoption," he told me. We talked in his three-room vacation suite in Las Vegas's Frontier Hotel. A waiter interrupted our discussion to deliver a platter of chilled seafood, bottles of liquor and mix for Burns's entourage. He knows how to live well.

"Adoption has a bad name," he continued. "They've been investigating me for years. The fact I'm still walking around says something."

What it says is that Burns adheres to the law very carefully. He has always listed his fees, to the penny, on affidavits filed with the court and, under the old Florida law, changed in 1975, that was all an attorney was legally required to do. It didn't matter whether his legal fee was five hundred, five thousand or fifty thousand dollars, so long as it was reported accurately. Burns always did that.

Under the new Florida law, an attorney's fee is limited to five hundred dollars for adoptions unless he can justify a higher fee to the court. To his credit, Burns has continued to handle adoptions under these circumstances, though, since the law now requires that both babies and adoptive parents be Florida residents, his volume has been cut down drastically. He expects the new law to be ruled unconstitutional soon, however, and he may be right. Some Florida law-enforcement officials have told me they have the same expectation.

Burns says his interest in adoption stems from his own family. He has three children, two of whom are adopted. He got into the adoption business in the mid-1960s. "I had a client for whom I'd handled an accident case. His daughter became pregnant. I really didn't know what to do. I researched it and did the adoption as a favor to help her out.

"And then she brought in another girl and somebody else brought in somebody else. Not to blow my own horn, but I really do treat these girls nice. I go out of my way to cater to them. If it weren't for the girls, I wouldn't have two-thirds of my family."

The pregnant girls and women who come to Burns are generally referred to him by word of mouth, some by physicians, some by other attorneys, and some by friends. A few have used Burns before and return to Florida a second time. He gives them rent, grocery money, and pays their medical bills.

Some years ago, Burns was criticized by the press and

police for running what they termed a "baby farm"—a house where as many as eight or nine pregnant girls at a time would stay under the supervision of a housemother. He no longer has the house because he does not have enough pregnant girls at one time to justify its expense.

"Let me tell you about the home," he said. "Initially, the maintenance costs for the girls were so astronomical that the judges would say to me, 'You know, your costs are very high.' I documented them. I realized other attorneys were getting the money in cash and not documenting expenses, but everything I had I documented—which is the way it should be.

"So when I had a few girls, I would put them in a house where they would share all expenses and, therefore, the expenses were cut—probably in half. I'd pay one electric bill, one water bill, and so on. Then, of course, the judges didn't complain; they were very happy.

"But along come the media and they blew the home up out of proportion as a baby farm. You're damned if you do and you're damned if you don't. I didn't have the girls scrubbing floors. They all had chores to do, but it was voluntary on their part. I treated them like human beings."

Burns likes to contrast his situation with what he says takes place at some of the adoption agencies, particularly those sponsored by one of the major religious groups.

"I've had girls come to me from the agencies where they were grossly mistreated," he said. "Not only had they paid sixty to eighty dollars a week to the charity, but they had to scrub floors. They ate tuna fish and garbage. They couldn't have a radio in their rooms. The supervision was so strict they felt guilty about everything they'd ever done. I've got it all documented. I've had mothers who've told me I saved their lives; they were about to crack up.

"Then these agencies charge the adoptive parents too. Because they're institutions, they were able to take money from both sides. If I did that, I would get arrested and be disbarred."

Burns says he is performing a service both to the natural mother and to the adoptive parents. The problem comes when one considers that he is the only representative of three interested parties—the adoptive parents, the natural mother, and the baby. When the adoptive parents are paying his fee, how can he honestly consider the welfare of the natural mother and her baby if they have a conflict of interest with the adoptive parents?

Burns told the 1975 Senate Subcommittee on Children and Youth that he considers himself the representative of the adoptive parents, but that he also considers the welfare of the natural mother and baby. Then-Senator Walter F. Mondale, who chaired that subcommittee, asked Burns, "If there is a conflict of interest between what the [adoptive] parents want and the best interests of the child, in whose favor do you decide?"

"I have never had such a conflict," Burns replied. "I do not understand what possible conflict there would be. The child is getting a home. . . ."

Though Burns claims to have met every parent who has adopted through his services, that contention is not borne out by the facts. The Subcommittee questioned Burns about a Cleveland couple who had adopted a baby through him. Their total cost for all services was approximately nine thousand dollars, $4779 of which was Burns's legal fee. He had never met the couple.

MONDALE: You represented parents in Cleveland whom you had not met. They paid a fee. How did you know you were acting in the best interests of the baby when you did not know the parents with whom you were placing him?

BURNS: From the letters and the conversations and telephone calls, I knew that the parents would give the baby a great deal of love and affection.

M: How did you know that?

B: From the letters and conversations with them.

M: From letters from them?

B: And conversations with them.

M: Did you believe they would reveal any problems they might have?

B: Well, it is similar to an interview that perhaps an agency would give to prospective parents.

M: Agencies go into the home and do other things, do they not?

B: Yes, which they also do in Florida and many other states prior to placement, but all states do it.

M: You do not see any possibility of a conflict of interest here?

B: As far as the child goes?

M: The child, the mother, the adopting parents.

B: I advise the adopting parents of the entire background of the girl. I try to give the girl information, without giving the names of the parents—some of the girls do not want to know the background and refuse to listen. Some do want to know the background.

M: I find it hard to believe you when you say you are protective of the baby's and the pregnant mother's interests since you do not know the parents who are going to adopt the child and you get a fee from them.

B: I have to rely on all the criteria that I have available to me.

M: But the information you receive is supplied by the parents who want the baby. Do you really believe they will provide their lawyer with information which might undermine their abilty to get the baby they want so badly? Does that make sense to you?

Apparently, it did make sense to Robert Burns. He still fails to see any possibility of a conflict of interest in his situation.

Burns claims to take a great deal of trouble to "counsel" the pregnant girls who stay with him. One thing on which they receive no counseling, however, is whether or not to keep their babies. Burns expects them to have made a firm decision to give their babies up for adoption before they come to him.

"I tell the girls, if they're vacillating, 'Go home and think it over. Don't sign any papers with me.' I don't want a girl who vacillates," he told me.

Burns claims "about ten" of the girls he has supported during their pregnancies have later decided to keep their babies. "There was only one girl who did that after birth," he said. "The others did it prior to going to the hospital, so I had enough time to contact the [prospective adoptive] parents. It's a horrible thing to call the parents and say, 'Your child has been born, but the girl changed her mind.' "

Burns's counseling centers around such matters as guilt about the pregnancy and birth control, topics not usually discussed by other attorneys in the business. He stressed that he puts in a great deal of time with each girl, sometimes merely being available when needed.

"More then [prior to the new legislation] than now, the girl would be from somewhere else," he told me. "She needed somebody. She had nobody. Four or five calls a day, I would have to go over there, see the girl, counsel her. It's not only a physical thing for a girl giving birth in that kind of situation, it's mental too."

The number of hours spent is one of the things which determined his fee before the five-hundred-dollar limit was set. "You have no idea what an adoption entails," Burns told me. "First of all, the girls have your home number. They can, and do call you at three o'clock in the morning with something imagined or real. A person handling an adoption who doesn't make at least three thousand to thirty-five hundred dollars is not breaking even. He isn't making anything for himself."

Burns, however, was making plenty. In testimony before the Senate Subcommittee on Children and Youth, he said that, for the past few years, adoption had constituted only one to one-and-a-half percent of his law business. He is basically a criminal lawyer. In documentation later supplied to that Subcommittee, however, Burns admitted having made $43,094.54 in adoption legal fees in 1973 and $57,715.69 in 1974. Given those figures, Vermont Senator Robert T. Stafford asked him if he wished to change his testimony about the percentage of his business attributed to adoption. Burns declined, though he allowed it might be closer to the one-and-a-half percent figure.

"On that basis, we should suggest that maybe the IRS will multiply that figure by ninety-eight point five percent and thereby estimate the balance of your income," Stafford suggested.

Burns's answer was, "Senator, the only thing I can say is now you can see why people do not want to testify."

If the $57,715.69 Burns made from adoptions in 1974 really constituted only one-and-a-half percent of his law income, then that total income would have had to be in the neighborhood of $3.8 million for that year.

The couples who have dealt with Burns evidently do not mind paying him the large sums. To Burns's credit, a few who could not afford large fees have been given babies for smaller sums or no fee at all.

"I have given babies to policemen, firemen—I'm a retired fireman myself—to people from all walks of life," Burns said. "Wealthy people, moderate people, that is not my criteria. I was brought up during the depression and my people made it."

But when Burns was asked if he considered himself a Robin Hood figure—in making the rich subsidize adoptions for the less well-to-do—he said he did not. And he further denied that a couple offering him a large sum would tempt him to lean their way.

"I've been offered fifteen thousand, twenty thousand dollars," he said. "I'd just reject anybody who offered me that kind of money. I would reject them on a psychological basis because I don't think they'd make good parents."

The adoptive parents pay all of the maintenance and medical expenses for the girl with whom Burns pairs them. And he tries, in pairing a pregnant girl with a couple, to match probable physical appearance.

"I match up children with parents the best that I can," he said. "It isn't a matter of chronological order. I tell the parents that. The main thing is coloring." Burns's sensitivity to physical appearance stems from his own experience. "When my adopted daughter came she was blonde." Burns is dark. "Insensitive clods would ask us, 'Who's blonde in your family?' They meant well, but they were insensitive." He tries to avoid having the same thing happen to couples who adopt through him. Burns also rejects any girls who are pregnant by non-white fathers. He says he can find no homes for biracial infants.

The financial liability for a pregnant girl can backfire for some couples, because the money is payable even if the baby is not healthy at birth and even if the mother decides not to release it for adoption. Though both cases are rare with Burns, they have happened.

"I tell all adoptive parents that as far as costs go, it's as if they went into the hospital and had the baby. If the baby's fine, beautiful. If the baby's defective in any way, they would have to pay the bills if they were the natural parents, so too in this case.

"When a baby is unadoptable—as soon as the parents know it—it should go to the state. The parents have to pick up the initial costs though (i.e. costs incurred prior to the child's becoming a ward of the state).

"Other attorneys would still demand their fee; I don't, though I probably put in more time on such a case, especially during the time I have to check with the pediatrician daily about the progress of the child."

And what about a case where a girl decides to keep her baby after it is born?

"Again, I would take no fee," Burns said, "but all the bills are paid by the adoptive parents. The girl should pay them, but go chase her down and the news media would think you were an ogre."

If handling an adoption requires so much personal time and at present yields so small a financial return, why does Burns continue to do it?

One reason, of course, is that the Florida law may be declared unconstitutional any day and the fee spiral will be on again. Burns cites another motivation: "I'm basically a criminal attorney. I handle a lot of negligence, workmen's compensation, commercial law. I do most everything. Adoption gives me the greatest pleasure when it works out correctly. There's no phase of law that's more rewarding. In most every legal situation, there's a winner and a loser—except adoptions. The parent is helped, the girl is helped, so I just enjoy it very much when it works out."

Even in a situation where the adults involved are all happy, though—the adoptive parents have their longed-for baby, the natural mother is free to start her life over again, and the attorney has his fee and personal satisfaction—I still wonder about the child.

As Walter Mondale asked: Who's representing the baby?

WALTER LEBOWITZ

In the summer of 1973, Miami Beach attorney Walter Lebowitz was arrested and charged with seven counts of buying and selling children. He was specifically accused of selling a week-old infant to a New Jersey engineer and his schoolteacher wife for seven thousand dollars.

That fall, Lebowitz was acquitted of the charges against him. The court ruled that the fees Lebowitz charged were legitimate adoption expenses, even though testimony at the trial held that the New Jersey couple had, in the back seat of a car, exchanged seven thousand dollars in traveler's checks for the child.

Lebowitz acknowledges having "placed" more than

forty infants, but denies "selling" them. "I charge high legal fees," he said, though he refuses to discuss just how high. "My fee is a personal thing. The 1966 Lee *v.* Buchanan case in Florida said an attorney can charge anything he likes." According to Martin Dardis, chief investigator for the Dade County State's Attorney's Office and the man who made the arrest, Lebowitz is not presently handling adoptions.

When Lebowitz was in business, he was among the most blatant of the baby brokers, going so far as to tell the news media he planned to write his autobiography and title it *The Baby Seller*. Sharon Horner once called him, having received his name a possible source of adoptable babies for both her own family and her group.

"I heard about this lawyer [Lebowitz] in Florida," she told me. "I called him as a representative of the group. He was so nice on the phone, very fatherly. He told me right up front his fee was ten thousand dollars, no questions asked. He really got my curiosity up."

Mrs. Horner's function with the Adoptive Parents Group was to screen adoption attorneys and steer group members toward lawyers who handled adoptions for what the group considered a legitimate fee and away from those who appeared to be profiteers. She decided to find out more about Lebowitz's operation and expressed interest in one of his babies.

"He said he would send me some papers, and sent me—besides the girl's name and address and her mother's, which is very unethical—everything about her. Things which, if I were adopting her child, I would want to know so I'd have more information to give the child someday."

What Lebowitz did not put in writing, however, was the ten-thousand-dollar price tag he had quoted. "He wrote telling me he'd take fifteen hundred dollars by check and 'the rest' in cash," Mrs. Horner said, "but he did not say how much that was. I was hoping he would put it in writing."

What was the money for? "He explained [over the phone] where every penny of that ten grand was going," she said, "every penny of it. He explained it all so that, if you did not know the situation, you would have believed him."

Sharon Horner, however, had talked with so many baby brokers that she knew the situation forward and backward. Her contact with Lebowitz angered her.

"I wanted to follow it up and do something about it, but I wasn't sure what. I called him again and told him I was having some trouble cashing in some bonds, that he'd receive my money in another month."

About this time, Mrs. Horner was contacted by John Farrell, a Dade County detective investigating babyselling, and she told him about her contacts with Walter Lebowitz. When Farrell came to Philadelphia, he asked her to place another call from her home there to the attorney in Florida while he listened on an extension phone. She agreed to do so.

Their ploy did not result in any usable evidence against Lebowitz though. "I don't know if the guy knew there was someone else on the phone or what, but that was the first time he would not give the price," she said. "He would not say the amount."

Another thing Mrs. Horner found strange about the Lebowitz deal was that he apparently did not have a connection with a Philadelphia attorney and wanted her to arrange one for him. "He told me I had to get a lawyer here and that I'd have to pay him but not to tell him that I also paid Lebowitz a fee. He would talk to my lawyer himself about fees. In other words, I'd have two lawyers' fees plus I guess he was hoping he could work a deal off the other lawyer too—so he could get another grand or so. My mouth fell open!"

Sharon Horner was not asked anything about her background and credentials as an adoptive parent. Though Lebowitz told reporters that he conducts background checks on his clients, there is significant evidence to the contrary, much of it given in testimony at his trial.

"The news media think there is something sinister about a private attorney playing God," he said, "deciding which couple to place a newborn infant with. I think an attorney is more qualified or at least *as* qualified as some clerk who works in a public agency.

"I pick the people with the most secure background, the best educational background and ability to provide the child with necessities and advantages."

Evidently he can tell all that by whether or not the couple in question can pay his legal fee. I wonder if their moral character and ability to love and care for a child can also be recognized by a peek at their bank balance?

SEYMOUR KURTZ

One of the most convoluted adoption agency-foundation-corporation chains in the world may be the one run by Chicago attorney and adoption entrepreneur Seymour Kurtz.

The forty-seven-year-old Kurtz heads—and in some cases is the sole staff for—five agencies, foundations, and corporations in Illinois, Delaware, Mexico, and the Netherlands. He currently plans expansion into at least one more unidentified state, the South American country of Colombia, and a second European country whose name he could not yet disclose.

There seems to be no logical reason for this complicated structure, though at least one government agency thinks it may offer a unique opportunity for babyselling, hiding profits, and operating without any effective government regulation. Adoption applications and funds are shuffled between foundations, agencies, and corporations—and between the United States and foreign countries—with an apparently needless amount of paperwork and confusion.

Although Kurtz claims his typical adoption costs only twenty-two hundred dollars plus transportation to Mexico, and that he loses money on his operation, his own literature contradicts him. A brochure he distributed to prospective adoptive parents cites typical costs of an adoption, including legal fees, at close to seven thousand dollars.

The Kurtz operation begins with Easter House in Chicago, a not-for-profit adoption agency, which has been licensed by the State of Illinois since 1962. Another Chicago link, Tzyrl Foundation, uses the same street address as Easter House. The former is listed as a tax-exempt, charitable organization with the Illinois Attorney General's office, but not with the Internal Revenue Service. Tzyrl's only function is to transfer paperwork and money to the Mexican branch of Kurtz's tree.

The Mexican agency, Casa del Sur, operating from Juarez and Mexico City, presently supplies almost all the babies for adoption. Kurtz said he was in the midst of changing this agency's name because "the old Mexican government expired at the end of last year and the new government came in with a new staff." The agency and its locations will remain precisely the same; only the name will change. Casa del Sur has been in existence since 1973.

Stichting [Foundation] Susu is Kurtz's Netherlands branch, named after his daughter Susan. Like Tzyrl, its only known purpose is to transfer applications and money to Casa del Sur, though some American couples making application to the Dutch agency were under the mistaken impression that they were going to get a European baby. Stichting Susu is essentially a post-office box. At one time Kurtz rented an office to go with it, but there is no evidence that the agency ever had any staff other than Kurtz himself. His involvement with Stichting Susu consisted of flying to The Hague to pick up the mail.

The final operational link in Kurtz's chain is a for-profit corporation based in Delaware, Suku Corporation, again named for Susan Kurtz. A state government official told me of fears that profits could be channelled to Suku Corporation as a way of getting around the non-profit status of Easter House and Tzyrl Foundation. "He [Kurtz] has created such jurisdictional problems that no one can get their teeth into them. He's all over the map," the official said.

Kurtz, however, says that his group of organizations is perfectly legal and ethical and that his only motivation is to help couples adopt babies and "offer an alternative to abortion." He fancies himself an incurable romantic, the kind of man Americans have trouble understanding.

"It's easier for Latins," he said. "In Mexico, they have an appreciation of a Don Quixote situation; many people who've helped us in Mexico share the same feeling I have—that this is an opportunity where we can logically and objectively render services to people who have great need and don't want to see their children destroyed in the womb."

Kurtz said he has received official scrutiny and unfavorable publicity only because he is the victim of an attempt by a former employee, Millicent Smith, and the Illinois Department of Children and Family Services to steal his business and ruin his reputation. He has filed lawsuits against both.

Kurtz claims that Millicent Smith, who was his Executive Director at Easter House for more than ten years, quit without notice around January 1, 1975, and opened her own agency, using both the Easter House name and files. He further alleges that she spent some sixty thousand dollars of Easter House money for her personal use and that he was unable to gain restitution in Illinois because of Ms. Smith's many friends in high political offices.

Millicent Smith's version is quite different. She no longer works in adoptions and refuses to discuss Seymour Kurtz.

In mid-1976, however, she talked with a reporter from the *Chicago Sun-Times* about the controversy. She told the reporter that, until 1973, Kurtz paid little attention to Easter House, that its adoptions were completely ethical and that their average cost was twenty-five hundred dollars. Then, she said, Kurtz came under financial pressure, including tax liens against him by the IRS. He unveiled his Mexican adoption agency plan, which Ms. Smith described. Adoptive parents who called Easter House were told to write to Stichting Susu in Holland, described as an adoption organization with affiliates around the world. "The truth was," she said, "the agency in The Hague was a post-office box . . . it has no personnel." The only agency Stichting Susu ever dealt with was Casa del Sur in Mexico, which in turn, would contact the adopting couple to tell them that Easter House would be conducting a home study at a fee of one hundred and fifty dollars.

The *Sun-Times* quoted Ms. Smith: "I couldn't understand why he was going this circuitous route to do the same thing we were already doing. It didn't make any sense to send couples all the way to Holland and have them wind up back here with us anyway. . . . He said it was a tax shelter, a way of getting money out of the city."

Ms. Smith also told the newspaper that Kurtz had instructed his Easter House employees to process the adoption applications quickly so they could collect the one-hundred-and-fifty dollar fee on each one as well as a "kickback" on legal fees.

When Kurtz was asked what logic there was in having five organizations do work which could be done by, at the most, one or two, he said, "You have no idea what the State of Illinois is doing with Easter House. If you were me, and you were involved with that kind of antagonism, would you put all your functions into one corporation?"

His diversification, however, dates from a good two years before the "antagonistic" events began. Illinois has jurisdiction over only Easter House and Tzyrl Foundation and has subjected both to scrutiny in the past two years. Kurtz complained in mid-1977 that he was about to undergo this third investigation by the Department of Children and Family Services. This latest inspection, he claimed, was prompted by the department's receipt of an anonymous letter saying Kurtz was "doing bad things."

"We've been investigated thoroughly twice in eight months and approved both times. Now, all of a sudden, we're being reinvestigated on an anonymous letter? You don't have to be a lawyer to see what they're up to. Fortunately, there are federal courts where you can get a certain amount of protection. I'll just have to file another lawsuit."

Thomas Felder, of the Department of Children and Family Services, confirms an interest in Kurtz's operation, but denies any harassment. When asked whether Illinois officials were interested in Kurtz's complicated chain of agencies, foundations, and corporations, Felder replied, "You better believe it. That is under investigation even as of now. It's been under continuous investigation—by the department and at various times by the State's Attorney of Cook County. Some inquiries have been made by the Attorney General of the State of Illinois—but not any in-depth inquiry. Some other questions have been posed by elements of the federal government as to whether or not this is a legitimate operation, whether it's licensed by the state, and other questions such as that."

Another argument Kurtz uses to justify the existence of his five links is that each is necessary because it has a unique function, which he considers legitimate and logical.

He says, first of all, that Easter House exists for the purpose it has always had: to do home studies and to place children for adoption. He admits that the agency places very few children at the present time, but mainly blames Millicent Smith and the Department of Children and Family Services for this.

"We placed about twenty or twenty-five a year before Ms. Smith left," he said. "But she took a number of our pregnant ladies and about a hundred files or so with home studies. Since then our business has fallen substantially. With all that going on, I think this year we'll have four or five adoptions."

Most of the scrutiny has revolved around Easter House's license. That agency's trouble seems to have started when Ms. Smith resigned. She had been employed as Executive Director of Easter House and held a master's degree in social work. Every adoption agency in Illinois is required to have such a staff member in order to keep its license. When Ms. Smith quit, Kurtz was technically in violation of Illinois's licensing requirements, according to Felder. The basic requirements for a license to operate an adoption agency in Illinois include having "a governing body—mainly that amounts to a board of directors; an executive director who is a qualified social worker—an MSW [master's in social work] with three to five years of experience; and the ability to show financial resources and solvency to provide services for the children that they're accepting for care."

In early 1975, the department sent notice to Kurtz that his license would not be reissued because of his staff deficiencies.

Felder explained, "In early 1975 Kurtz did not meet the requirements because he did not have an executive director and, indeed, had no agency staff as far as the department was aware. Agencies are required to notify us of their staff, their qualifications, and any changes occurring in that grouping. Kurtz did not, as far as our records show, have any staff whatsoever."

Felder said that, beyond the executive director and an approved board of directors, his department requires no specific number of staff for an adoption agency. Interestingly, though, four of the nine directors listed in Easter House's 1975 annual report said they were not asked to serve and did not know they were listed as directors. Under those circumstances they could hardly have been doing much "directing."

When Kurtz replaced Millicent Smith with another MSW, Felder said, his license was reissued.

A disturbing deficiency in Illinois adoption law is that

there is no provision requiring an agency to be not-for-profit. If a person, or group of persons, meets the stated criteria, the Department of Children and Family Services is obligated to issue a license. When Millicent Smith applied for a license for her for-profit agency and met the requirements, one was issued to her. She used the name Easter House Adoption Agency, Inc., which she claimed was not similar enough to Kurtz's Easter House to cause any confusion. The Secretary of State agreed with her and issued a license in that name.

Kurtz maintains that the Department of Children and Family Services should have forced Ms. Smith to use a different name, but Felder says they did not have that authority.

Kurtz's second Chicago organization, Tzyrl Foundation, has a somewhat fuzzier purpose than Easter House. Kurtz explained, "Tzyrl is not an adoption agency. It does not place children for adoption. It does communicate information to people interested in adoption. It facilitates things as much as possible; it gets their applications; it helps collect information and passes it on to the Mexican institution. And it underwrites the cost of the function of the Latin American institution."

Where does Tzyrl get its money? Mainly, from American couples who adopt Casa del Sur babies, Kurtz said. He also claims to have put in his own money to the tune of a quarter of a million dollars. He says he has a separate income from his law practice and has used that income to make loans to Tzyrl.

In 1973 and 1974, Tzyrl Foundation filed federal income-tax returns as a tax-exempt organization, but it was not registered with the IRS as tax-exempt. Kurtz said this was merely an accountant's error and didn't make any difference anyway because Tzyrl had made no money.

The reason it made no money was that it paid sixteen thousand dollars for Kurtz's travel bills (mostly air fares to Holland to pick up Stichting Susu's mail) and sixty-one thousand to Casa del Sur to cover that agency's operating costs.

Why didn't Easter House perform the relatively easy work of Tzyrl? Why was a second entity needed? Kurtz replied, "Both of these functions under one roof is a management problem I don't care to have."

"Under one roof" was an unfortunate choice of terminology because both *are* literally under one roof—the one over 111 North Wabash in Chicago. They do, however, remain separate organizations.

Kurtz elaborated, "As we get bigger and bigger, the function of each entity will be more and more removed from the other. I don't want to have social workers at Easter House concerning themselves with communicating information about Mexico."

The third of Kurtz's organizations, Stichting Susu, functions for Europe the way Tzyrl Foundation functions for the United States. There was no explanation of why Americans' adoption applications were sent to Holland, leading many couples to believe that they would adopt a European, not a Mexican, baby.

Kurtz has now decided that the work of Stichting Susu can be done from the United States and he will soon dissolve the Netherlands organization. "I think at this point I can do the whole thing from this hemisphere without going to Europe," he said. "Those trips were exhausting for me. We're getting in an amount of applications from Europe without the requirement of Stichting Susu, so there's no sense having a duplicate set of offices, personnel, what have you."

The personnel were more than duplicates; they were

the same. The staff of both foundations consisted of Seymour Kurtz.

In his next breath, after describing his plan to dissolve the Holland organization because it is unnecessary, Kurtz described a plan to open another just like it in a different European country. He declined to name the country, but said this organization would be different in one important way: "Stichting Susu was established in Holland, but without the government's participation as a sponsor. We are negotiating with another government in Europe that will sponsor our activity . . . we will work with them and for them in this."

Somehow the logic of discontinuing one organization in Holland because the work can be handled in Illinois and then starting another like it in a second European country because the government there will be a participant seems vague. The babies available for adoption will still be Latin American, not European. Casa del Sur, Kurtz's Mexican adoption agency, is the baby source at the present time for applicants to Tzyrl and Susu.

Latin America is an adoption entrepreneur's utopia. As Kurtz admits, "In Latin America, they don't have licensing and they don't have any law governing adoption agencies. All you really have to do is create your corporation and engage in its purpose."

In existence since 1973, Casa del Sur has placed about four hundred babies for adoption, about three hundred of them in Mexican families. Those adopted by Mexican families tend to be the ones with Indian features and rather dark complexions; the lighter ones go to Americans and Europeans, a fact that has led to charges of racism against Kurtz.

He defends his position, though, saying, "The babies are placed by what's best for the baby. We take into consideration their coloring and their anthropological features, the biological background—as much as can be discerned—and the applicant parents. So, in fact, if a child has Indian characteristics, with Aztec features, then that child is placed in a home where he would look normal, natural. He is not placed with Scandinavians in Minnesota."

Most social workers, however, want to be absolutely sure a couple adopting a child of another race will respect that baby's origins and not try to pretend those origins aren't real. Placing a light-complected Mexican child with a white couple who really want a white baby may mean heartache for all involved. But if a couple has honestly accepted the fact that the child will look different than they do, will be of another race, does it matter if the skin is a bit lighter or darker?

While the American and European couples adopting through Casa del Sur pay a substantial fee, adoptions are free for Mexican families. "We accept donations from them which usually amount to approximately five percent of our operating costs," Kurtz said. "All the rest of the operating costs for Casa del Sur come from Tzyrl Foundation."

Casa del Sur's expenses include maintenance costs for the pregnant girls and women and medical costs for the delivery of their babies. These costs, however, are much lower than for comparable services in the United States. For example, typical medical expenses for a pregnancy would be only about one hundred and twenty dollars in Mexico, as compared with eight hundred or more in the U.S.

The final Kurtz link which exists at this writing is Suku Corporation, a for-profit organization based in Delaware. Kurtz said it "functions as a liaison and clerical service" between adoptive parents, Casa del Sur, and the Mexican courts. He refers adoptive parents to a specific group of lawyers in the United States. The couples pay a legal fee of nine hundred dollars each, but the lawyers keep only ninety dollars. The remaining eight hundred and ten dollars go to Suku Corporation.

What is done with that money?

Kurtz explained: "Suku then pays fees to lawyers in Mexico who handle the Mexican court's portion of the transactions and its Delaware staff who do almost all of the clerical work in amassing a file that's, perhaps, two or three inches thick with documentation."

Kurtz said that the amount of legal paper work involved in one of his Mexican adoptions is staggering. "In the first adoption we did in Mexico, I did all the legal work. I wouldn't do that again for ten thousand dollars," he said. Evidently he won't have to. He's found some other lawyers who will do the entire American half for only ninety dollars.

Kurtz currently plans to expand into the Colombian adoption market, one that has grown as a source of babies for American families in recent years. "In the next three or four weeks," he said with evident pride, "I expect to be in Bogota, where the Cardinal and I are both founders of an institution." Apparently some factions of the Catholic Church do indeed support him, as he claims.

Tzyrl will be the United States liaison with the as-yet-unnamed Colombian adoption agency, as well as for Casa del Sur under its new name. Kurtz also plans expansion into at least one more state in the United States. Again, he declined to identify his target.

When asked why, in a situation where there are already so few babies available for adoption and far too many adoption agencies figuratively fighting over them, he would want to open still another agency, he replies that he thinks agencies not only have the power to accept girls who want to give up their babies for adoption, but the obligation to make their services known to these girls as well. Existing agencies, in Kurtz's opinion, have failed to do this. The result, he says, is that there are girls having abortions because they don't know they could give birth and have their babies adopted. "I am confident that there are thousands of American babies being deprived of life, being deprived of good homes," he said, "only because their unsophisticated young mothers don't know what the community has available to them."

Considering Seymour Kurtz's shrewdness and inventiveness it is likely he will get the chance to tell these mothers exactly what "the community" has available for those in their particular situation.

JOSEPH SPENCER

Tiny, silver-haired septuagenarian Joseph Spencer has sometimes been called the Dean of Independent Adoption. His New York-based business has been thriving for more than twenty-five years.

Over the past few years Spencer has been profiled by several journalists posing as prospective adoptive parents. Thus the picture that emerges in regard to this man is, perhaps, the clearest of all. The first such newspaper profile of Spencer was researched by two *New York Times* reporters, who phoned Spencer in early 1973. He told them he was so busy he could not see them for at least six weeks. He added that he charged one hundred dollars for an hour's consultation and that the couple would probably have to wait at least two years for a baby. "The situation is grim," was his summary.

When the "husband" indicated that money was no

object, Spencer told him, "Well, I do take certain cases in my home in Jackson Heights." An appointment was set up for the following week.

Two days later, Spencer called the couple and told them a Philadelphia lawyer who usually handles babies from Greece, Italy, and Yugoslavia knew of an American baby about to be born. The cost would be ninety-five hundred dollars plus twenty-five hundred for Spencer, a total of twelve thousand dollars.

"If you're not interested," he said, "we can still have the meeting on Monday." He confirmed the Monday appointment the next day in a letter, which also informed the couple that Spencer's fee for an hour's consultation had risen to two hundred and fifty dollars. They canceled the appointment.

The next week, one of the reporters (who Spencer did not know was one of the *Times* reporters who had contacted him) interviewed him in his office. Spencer refused to discuss his fees, saying only, "When you go to the best, you pay more. That's why Louis Nizer can command five-thousand-dollar fees and why I get more than other people."

Spencer said he did not consider himself among the group of profiteering attorneys involved in adoptions; in fact, he said, he abhorred their practices, but admitted he often dealt with them when he had a client desperate for a baby. "Money talks in this business," he said. "It's gotten to the point where babies that are supposed to go to my clients are being snatched right out from under our noses for more money. There's a terrific hunger out there. The people who will suffer are those in the fifteen- to sixteen-thousand salary bracket or less, because they'll never be able to afford to adopt—unless they have wealthy parents."

Two years later, Spencer was contacted by a reporter

from the *Cleveland Plain Dealer,* also posing as a prospective adoptive parent. He told this reporter that the costs of adopting a baby would depend on the type of child being sought.

"It can run as little as twenty-five hundred dollars if you want a Korean child, to a lot more," he said. "For a white Caucasian child at birth most lawyers quote substantial amounts, but even there it doesn't run much beyond thirteen thousand dollars."

Spencer said he could deliver a child in as little as one month. "Believe it or not," he told the reporter, "I have biographies of mothers who are going to give birth this month and for the next two months. So, if you should be pleased with any of these biographies and if the attorney who sent them to me has confirmed the fact that they are still available, then we process."

In a later interview with the *Plain Dealer,* Spencer denied that the cost of adoptions he arranges goes as high as thirteen thousand dollars. He declined to say what his legal fees totaled and would not reveal how many adoptions he handles yearly.

In 1976, the *Chicago Sun-Times'* Pam Zekman (pretending to be looking for a baby to adopt) also contacted Spencer.

"What kind of child are you seeking?" he asked her. "Do you want a white newborn infant or would you be interested in a [racially] mixed or Korean child? Those are easier to get, you know. It is very difficult to get a healthy white newborn child."

Spencer was frank with Ms. Zekman when she asked about costs. "Most of the children come through other lawyers, who are like middlemen. So, besides the hospital costs and the living costs for the mother, there would be a finder's fee—which is called a legal fee—to the other lawyer for his services. Actually, it *is* a finder's fee because he will help us find a baby, but we can't call it that.

"Now an adoption that is handled in that manner— which yours would most likely be—could run as high as fourteen thousand dollars."

New York adoption judges and other authorities questioned by Ms. Zekman and other *Sun-Times* reporters said that adoption costs of fourteen thousand dollars seemed exorbitant.

Two reporters who investigated Spencer's operation both from the outside and the inside were Lynne McTaggart of the *New York Daily News* and Bernard Gavser of NBC-TV. They had decided to look into the New York baby market to see just what went on when one approached it looking for a child. "We got into it because Bernie wanted to do something on adoption for his station," Ms. McTaggart began. "He asked me to help him out, and I agreed."

They posed as a couple seeking an adoption at any price. At the time of their charade, Ms. McTaggart was a twenty-three-year-old Catholic; Gavser a fifty-three-year-old Jew. In order to see if there was anything even vaguely resembling an agency screening connected with black-market adoption, they even added a few more liabilities to their biographies.

"We decided to say that Bernie had three children by a prior marriage and that he had a vasectomy before divorcing his wife," Ms. McTaggart explained. Agencies frown on people who have voluntarily sterilized themselves and also favor childless couples. So, with their religious and age differences, the fact that Gavser already had children and had been sterilized, this couple would have been an instant reject at almost any adoption agency.

The only qualification with which they armed themselves was their ability to support a child. "We said Bernie was a free-lance film producer with a forty-two-thousand-dollar income and I was a self-employed literary agent making twenty-one thousand in commissions." Ms. McTaggart raised her age to twenty-seven to make her income sound more plausible. They added substantial investments in land and Broadway plays to their portfolio and claimed to have a New York City apartment and a house in New Jersey.

The fictitious Mr. and Mrs. Gavser were prime candidates for a high-priced adoption. They obviously had no place else to turn if independent adoption did not work for them, and they could afford a lot of money to get their baby.

When they called Spencer's office, an associate told them—over the phone—that they could expect to pay between six thousand and twelve thousand dollars for a baby. Soon after, they received a note asking for a one-hundred-dollar consultation fee before Spencer would even see them to discuss a possible adoption.

When the Gavsers met Spencer, it was at his home in Jackson Heights. Ms. McTaggart described the meeting in her article: "We rang and a little old man with a wizened, bony face and long, silver-gray hair opened the door and introduced himself as Joseph Spencer. He wore a bright orange velour turtleneck, imitation suede trousers and carpet slippers. He couldn't have been more than five-foot-one. He led us into his living room and said we'd have a bit of a wait since he was busy with other clients. But before he left us, he handed Bernie a sheet of paper. 'That is the biography of a young lady who is about to give birth in three weeks,' Spencer said. 'Is that too close for you? If it looks good to you, it's still available.' "

They looked the biography over. It was of a twenty-five-year-old former high-school cheerleader, five-foot-nine inches with auburn hair and fair complexion. She lived in Dallas and had a good job with an advertising agency. She was supposedly very pretty, extremely healthy and had never used drugs. The unborn baby's father was listed as a thirty-five-year-old married physician.

When the couple entered his office, Spencer showed them biographies of several more pregnant girls, but stressed that the Dallas woman was the best choice for them. "There is not a biography among the list as good as this," he told them. "This will be snapped up."

Spencer outlined his charges for the Gavsers. Ms. McTaggart's article reported the following:

> Obtaining the Dallas child, or any of the others would, he said, simply be a matter of our giving him the go ahead and a deposit, waiting for the birth, flying to Dallas to "pick up" and leaving the "rest" to him.
>
> "Now," Spencer said, continuing, "this would be a package of twelve thousand dollars. The lawyer there [in Dallas] gets the bulk of that and he gets it for everything, including all the things you would have to pay ordinarily—like hospital, doctor, pediatrician.
>
> "And today there is the common custom of giving the mother what we call a 'cost-of-living' allowance. It used to be illegal. . . . This custom has expanded, they're all indigent now; they all want money, and it's more than two, three, four, five hundred. So that runs into a thousand or two."
>
> I still didn't understand why, using Spencer's "preferable" way, we'd have to pay twelve thousand dollars plus the costs of a two-day stay in Dallas, or

why Spencer considered that a bargain rate. He explained that the Dallas attorney's price had dropped because he was down to the wire on the due date.

"Let me tell you," he said, "this middle-man, this lawyer we're going to deal with, charges what turns out to be a 'finder's fee.' He hasn't got a right to it. He should charge a legal fee. He does some legal work and he's entitled to a reasonable fee.

"He takes a chance. . . . You get an ordinary birth, it's one thing. You get a Cesarean, it's more. . . . He takes that chance, he gets what's left; it could be two, three, four thousand. . . . You're paying for insurance; you're paying for a certain amount of assurance."

Spencer's operation doesn't force the adoptive parents to pay if the infant is stillborn or born defective.

To further reassure the Gavsers, Spencer gave them the name and phone number of the Dallas attorney, Richard Goodner, and urged them to call him directly. Ms. McTaggart did so the next day, identifying herself as Mrs. Gavser. Goodner gave her substantially the same sales pitch about the expectant mother Spencer had and then detailed the costs of the adoption should they decide they wanted this baby.

He claimed that medical expenses would be about two thousand dollars, providing there were no unusual complications. In reality, two thousand dollars should cover quite a few complications. Though delivery and hospital costs vary a great deal in different cities, one thousand dollars should have covered medical expenses for a normal delivery at that time in even the most expensive case.

"Then," Goodner told Ms. McTaggart, "we had one other thing. She had an eight-hundred-dollar dental bill . . .

and she may or may not want me to give her some money. I don't know. She asked me—and I told her I didn't know, I didn't think I had it—but she asked me if I could possibly get her some money to buy clothes when I got through."

Money given to the natural mother for anything other than her medical and essential living expenses results in deception of the court. Often, though, attorneys will tell the adoptive parents the mother wants money.

Goodner said that the natural mother's cost for "up-keep and everything" had been between three thousand and six thousand dollars and they could likely plan to pay between nine thousand and ten thousand dollars total for the Texas end of the adoption. With Spencer's charges, that would bring it up to at least thirteen thousand dollars.

To further cement the bargain, Goodner referred the couple to a Dr. Holiday, who was to deliver the baby. Ms. McTaggart phoned him as well and he told her, "I would anticipate delivering a very normal baby. . . . It will be coming from very good blood lines and excellent parentage. . . . And I expect a very *pretty* baby." Dr. Holiday assured her that the mother would not decide to keep her baby, that he could tell, having been through several previous adoptions.

A week later, Spencer talked with Ms. McTaggart and asked whether or not they had decided to take the Dallas baby. "Another couple has made a bid on it," he said.

With enough material for their stories and at a critical point in the process, she told him she and her husband were not prepared to take a baby quite this soon, but they would be in touch with him again later.

Somehow, this whole thing sounds more like purchasing a pedigreed dog than adding a member to one's family. Ms. McTaggart said she found many aspects of the procedure depressing: the baby became a commodity, the natural mother merely breeding stock, and, as an "adoptive parent" in this kind of transaction, she felt her own humanity a bit reduced too.

In early 1977, Pam Zekman told me she had received a card from Spencer, addressed to her "adoptive parent" pseudonym, saying he was no longer handling adoptions. But when I called his New York office in April of that year I was assured by a secretary that Spencer was still in business. I was given an appointment to discuss adopting a baby in June, 1977, and, prior to that, received a letter confirming the appointment. The letter included a questionnaire to be filled out. Most of the questions pertained to financial status —employment, annual income, the size of my house or apartment, et cetera. At the top of the form was a disclaimer: "These questions are generally those you will be required to answer when a home study is made after you have custody of the child. Please bear in mind that I do not place children."

The letter also reminded me: "Please note that I charge a consultation fee of one hundred dollars payable before we meet. Check in the amount indicated should be forwarded to this office with the completed questionnaire before the date of our appointment."

The appointment was not kept, but I doubt that put a dent in Joseph Spencer's thriving business. Last I heard he still had more business than most septuagenarians could hope to handle.

STANLEY MICHELMAN

"It formally began five years ago, on October twenty-third. I'll never forget the date," Stanley Michelman said.

"My wife gave birth to our first child, and there I am at the hospital waiting for her to deliver while this girl I am supposed to be meeting is landing at the airport."

The "girl" was a pregnant woman Michelman was importing from Germany to give birth in New York. Her baby would be adopted by one of Michelman's clients.

"I sent a friend out there and paced the floor of the delivery room," he said, "looking at my watch, wondering if he made it. When my wife delivered, as soon as I knew she was safe, I rushed to the airport, but I couldn't find my friend.

"It's been like that ever since. Rushing around and around taking care of these things. I love it. Why, there are people I am supposed to be seeing right now in New York, but here I am in Chicago. I never unpack my suitcase. I am here today, gone tomorrow. I have to be there when a baby is delivered and I am everywhere."

Michelman was in a rare expansive mood about his adoption business because he thought he was talking to a pregnant ice skater, Patricia O'Malley, who would turn her baby over to him for adoption. In reality, Ms. O'Malley was Pam Zekman of the *Chicago Sun-Times*.

Though he claims to have bowed out of the adoption business in late 1976 Michelman "ran" a very successful operation for about six years.*

Michelman works with his brother, Harvey, also an attorney, in New York City. Harvey told Ms. Zekman that their firm of Michelman & Michelman has "represented people in two hundred or more adoptions." In a later inter-

---

* Stanley Michelman was indicted in October, 1977, by a Suffolk County, New York, grand jury "on grand larceny charges and social services law violations in connection with what was described as a baby-for-sale merchant." In February, 1978, he was indicted in Manhattan on 192 counts in connection with babyselling.

view, however, Stanley said his firm handled only about twelve adoptions per year which, over the five-year period he was discussing, would be only sixty—significantly fewer than his brother's estimate. A year earlier, Stanley Michelman had told the *Cleveland Plain Dealer* that he handled about thirty-six adoptions a year and made about ninety thousand dollars annually from his law practice.

Michelman is primarily known for his aggressiveness and creativity in finding pregnant women who will give up their babies for adoption. He has had referrals from many states as well as from Western Europe. He is also known for having these women sign an illegal, and worthless, agreement to repay all monies expended on their behalf if they decide not to relinquish their child.

One abortion service which has referred callers to Michelman is Abortion and Adoption Assistance, Inc., of Roslyn Heights, New York. Telephone books in at least fourteen cities in thirteen states—including Minneapolis, Cleveland, Chicago, New Haven, Tallahassee, Boston, New Orleans, and Louisville—list the number for Abortion and Adoption Assistance, Inc., which is run by Marilyn Sheldon, who claims she never received compensation for the referrals. Mrs. Sheldon is now referring potential adoptions to at least one other New York attorney.

A typical conversation with Mrs. Sheldon was reported in the *Plain Dealer*. She first asked the caller's name, marital status, length of employment and employer. Then she began to talk about the adoption of the child.

"You don't care to keep the baby and I assume you want to put the baby up for adoption and you want help with that . . .

"Now all your expenses can be paid . . . the hospital, the doctor, you know, the whole bit . . . the legal expenses . . . I mean, that's the least you can get."

The caller asked, "How about things like food and rent?"

"I'm sure that can be arranged," Mrs. Sheldon said. "The adoptive parents are the ones who pay the expenses.

"I will give you the telephone number of a terrific young man," she said. "You'll be crazy about him. He relates so well to young people. There are many people I could put you in touch with, but I think in your situation—with your schooling, you are a bright young lady—you will relate well to this young man. He's an attorney . . . he's young."

She supplied the name and phone number of Stanley Michelman.

Plain Dealer reporters called Mrs. Sheldon's service and told her they were pregnant women calling from Cleveland, Denver, New York City, St. Louis, and Minneapolis. She always referred them to Stanley Michelman.

Another reporter Marilyn Sheldon referred to Michelman was Lynne McTaggart of the *New York Daily News* who was still researching her story, this time posing as a pregnant unwed mother.

Mrs. Sheldon insisted that Michelman call Ms. McTaggart to discuss her "problem." He did so the next day.

"How are you feeling?" Michelman asked her.

"Not so good," she said.

"Marilyn told me all about you, Lynne, and I can assure you that all expenses will be taken care of—medical, hospital, doctor, all expenses incurred during pregnancy, like rent, food, clothing, if you need it. So when can you see me?"

"Marilyn was really wonderful," Ms. McTaggart told Michelman. "I was a mess when I called and she really calmed me down."

"Isn't she great?" he replied. "We work with her quite often."

Michelman's "work with Marilyn" consisted mainly of receiving the names and phone numbers of pregnant women, Ms. McTaggart later wrote.

Reporter McTaggart told Michelman she was twenty-three and a post-graduate student at the New School in Manhattan, studying drama. She claimed she was Catholic and "couldn't handle an abortion," but had been offered a scholarship to the Royal Academy of Dramatic Arts in London, so she couldn't keep her baby either. She said she worked part time as a waitress and took dancing lessons, which accounted for her slim profile, despite her claim to be three months pregnant.

On December 10, 1974, Ms. McTaggart changed her stylish work clothes for jeans and a shirt—what she called her "unwed mother outfit"—and went to call on Stanley Michelman.

She later wrote:

> There were four other people in the tiny waiting room and no available chairs. I dropped my bookbag on the floor and sat on it.
>
> I was called in first, escorted to Stanley's office and instructed to wait for him. The office had inexpensive shag carpeting, imitation walnut paneling, and modern art on the walls. Contents of files were strewn over the desk, window sill and corner filing cabinets.
>
> After a few minutes, Stanley Michelman burst

in, gave me a quick handshake and began to shuffle through the heaps of papers on his large desk.

He pulled out a six-page form and proceeded to ask me about my background, personality and health. He asked the same questions about my boy friend.

"How would you describe yourself as a person?" he asked as he scribbled the last answer on the form. "Outgoing?"

I nodded. "I guess."

"Any serious illness or hereditary diseases in the father's background?"

"I don't know that."

"I'll put down 'no.' "

We finished all six pages of the "confidential" interview in 10 minutes.

Michelman next pulled out the photostated form letter that, when signed by both of us, would be addressed from me to his law office. He handed me a pen and told me to sign it.

The letter began: "This letter is intended to confirm our understanding and agreement with regard to your placing my as of yet unborn child for adoption." It then said that I agreed to have the adoptive parents pay for all my pregnancy expenses; that I would pay them back if I failed to surrender the child; that Michelman was their attorney and I had decided not to seek counsel of my own.

I hesitated with the pen in my hand. The letter looked very precise and very legal. I figured it was the final step a mother takes to relinquish all rights to her child. I knew that I had to sign it to keep up the masquerade, but I wasn't sure exactly what I would be signing. For a few horrible moments, I believed that I would really have to come up with a baby. Or pay back exorbitant legal fees. I imagined myself, years from now, married, legitimately pregnant and running, with Michelman chasing after me, waving the letter furiously.

I signed the letter.

Michelman was scanning the application form. "I bet I could probably tell you already what parents you'd want," he said. "Let's see, I'd say you'd want . . . people who were educated? Intelligence is a big thing with you."

"Yeah," I said.

"Religion isn't a big consideration."

"Right."

"They'd have to be professional, well-off and, you know," he searched for a word, gesturing, 'artsy!' " He looked very pleased.

"Can I know things about them?"

"Oh, sure, I'll tell you all about them, their background, their looks, everything. In fact, I could show you the contract they sign. I'll just cover the names."

"Will I have proof that they'll take the baby?"

"Oh, sure, they sign a contract. Listen, normally we don't do this to the kids that come in here—16 and 17 years old—but for you . . . You seem to have a good head, you know, you seem to be together about yourself. I'll show you the contract and their papers."

With luck, Michelman said, he would "work out" something with the adoptive parents so I could know their names. But he refused a meeting.

Suddenly, Michelman remembered that I had

not been to a doctor. He gave me the name of one at Flower and Fifth Avenue Hospital on 106th St. and said he had a "credit card" there. He told me simply to sign his name to a bill. He said he'd set up an appointment, and I agreed to call the following day. He got up to escort me out, noticed something on his desk, and grabbed it from the top of one pile of papers.

"Say, how'd you like this couple for parents?" He tossed me a photograph.

The couple, probably in their late 30's, stood arm-in-arm in a living room, smiling for the camera. They looked hopeful.

Ms. McTaggart obviously could not keep the appointment with Michelman's doctor. She asked her own gynecologist to confirm she was his patient but refuse to give out information about her should anyone inquire about her. She then told Michelman she had gone to another doctor and gave him her gynecologist's name. Michelman accepted this change in plans and never, during the time reporter McTaggart dealt with him, called her doctor.

Michelman often reminded Ms. McTaggart to let him know if there was anything she needed. When she complained about her waitress job he told her she could work for him. "You can be a girl Friday around here. We just lost our last one because she delivered in May and went home to Kansas."

He said she could work as little or as much as she wished and that the job would not interfere with her classes. Ms. McTaggart accepted and, on January 8, took up a new observation post within the organization: she went to work for a colleague of Michelman's, Martin Jay Siegel. She received her first paycheck (for nine hours' work at three dollars an hour) on January 29, along with her first expense check for $210 to cover school tuition money. On Monday of the next week, he sent her a check for $225 to cover food and rent for the month.

Ms. McTaggart figured out what her "expenses" would total for the couple who would ultimately adopt her fictitious baby. She would be charging them for six months' rent, a total of twelve hundred dollars; food money for the same period, totaling six hundred; about one hundred and twenty dollars for phone bills; one hundred for clothing and drugs; one hundred for school supplies; at least another hundred for miscellaneous expenses; and about seventeen hundred in medical expenses.

"Added to the two hundred and ten dollars for classes, ten for TV rental in the hospital, and twenty for a post-delivery gift," she said, "the adoptive parents of my 'child' would have to pay $4160 on my expenses alone—and that's if I was relatively frugal."

She felt that, given Michelman's setup, the pregnant woman was the one who determined the final cost of the adoption and her expense account could easily be padded. Some of the "expenses" she claimed seemed hardly indispensable items, or even legitimately connected to pregnancy.

"In one instance," she said, "Michelman allegedly told an adoptive couple they would have a baby from Germany, but would have to anticipate paying for the boyfriend of the natural mother to visit her for a month in the United States."

An additional expense for couples who adopted the German and Austrian babies Michelman supplied was one hundred and seventy-five dollars paid to Ingrid, his "counselor." Ingrid earned her salary for "consultation and translation" of all adoption documents involving European women. "Along with translating the legal documents and conversing with the women," Ms. McTaggart found, "she [Ingrid] handles all of their expenses and ensures that there is a present, flowers, and a television set waiting at the hospital."

Ingrid was essential to Michelman because he had an active finders' service in West Germany, where the government had banned adoption by non-Germans. Michelman, however, was able to get around both that ban and any red tape involved with the immigration and naturalization of a foreign-born baby in this country in a simple, ingenious way. A Michelman operative contacted pregnant women within Germany and offered them all-expense-paid trips to New York during their eighth or ninth month of pregnancy. The women who agreed to the trip bore their babies in the United States. Thus the infants automatically became U.S. citizens, and were eligible for adoption here. Neither the German nor American governments had grounds to protest. (This was the same type of operation Ronald Silverton tried to set up in Yugoslavia and Great Britain.)

With her job in the Michelman organization, Reporter McTaggart was able to see its workings at close range. "I learned that one of Michelman's principal contacts is a Patricia Johnson," she said. "She oversees the first contact with the pregnant women, handles their expenses in West Germany, and submits to Michelman bills for their 'pickup.'

"My boss, Martin Siegel, an associate attorney, lists Michelman's New York address as his U.S. office and lists Patricia Johnson's address as his office abroad. At one point Patricia Johnson was apparently attempting to expand operations into France."

That wasn't the only expansion anticipated: "Michelman's plans," Ms. McTaggart said, "had him looking toward

Central and South America. He'd made contact with a Dr. Mabel Tsin in Buenos Aires and with a Dr. Joseph Younger in Guadalajara, Mexico, telling them that he had numerous clients anxious to adopt newborn infants. He suggested the doctors contact him if they were interested."

But even without expansion, Ms. McTaggart found, Michelman at one point during her employment with him had twenty-four pregnant women planning to give up their babies for adoption. Among them were five from Florida, two from West Germany, three from Ohio, and two from Georgia.

Ms. McTaggart spoke highly of Michelman's treatment of her. "I could call him at home at any time," she said. "He was generous and witty, even, at times, charming. He tried very hard to speak what he thought was my language, and to minimize what could have been the biggest jam of my life.

"But," she said, "I will never know if his goodness was genuine, because there was over ten thousand dollars at stake in the safe delivery of my baby."

Along with her $4160 in expenses, Michelman would have charged the adoptive couple his usual twenty-five-hundred-dollar legal fees. Ms. McTaggart also learned that Michelman had prepared a rider requiring the couple to deposit four thousand dollars with the firm of Michelman & Michelman prior to obtaining the baby. The money, the rider said, represented "the Associate's fee" and was payable "in cash."

That money, Ms. McTaggart reported, had bought the prospective parents of her child little to date. "They had no medical proof that mine was a normal pregnancy, no more of my background than a ten-minute interview, no proof of the father's health, no assurance that anything I said to Michelman had been true; no assurance, finally, that the father of the child, who was being written off as 'abandoned' to save paperwork, might not attempt to gain custody of the child."

For the adoptive parents, this deal had been a total gamble.

They lost.

In mid-February, Lynne McTaggart told Michelman she planned to visit a friend in Delaware for a few days. Then she had a friend who was a nurse call him and say she had just been released from Wilmington Medical Center where she had suffered a miscarriage.

In late February, Ms. McTaggart called Michelman and told him that, since he had been so good to her, she had decided to return his "expense" checks. She cashed the paychecks she had legitimately earned by working at Michelman & Michelman, however, and sent the money to New York State Senator Joseph Pisani, who was, at that time, investigating adoption law, as a contribution to further the cause of adoption reform.

It was, her note read, to be a "gift from Stanley Michelman."

The pregnancy of a woman like Lynne McTaggart would have represented an ideal situation for Michelman. She was not only attractive, intelligent, and well-educated, she was in New York.

At one time, Michelman maintained pregnant girls in their home towns, but that operation began running into trouble with local officials and hospitals in other states. After that, he brought almost all the girls to New York to give birth.

An example of this kind of trouble was reported in the *Plain Dealer*. On this particular occasion, Michelman had flown to Cleveland with a New York couple to pick up a child born at Deaconess Hospital. The situation made the hospital's administrator nervous, so he called Stanley R. Freeman of the Cuyahoga County Probate Court to come to the hospital.

Michelman produced New York State adoption papers, according to both Freeman and the hospital official, but was told those papers had no bearing on children in Ohio. Freeman said he asked Michelman to go to Probate Court and meet with a judge on the matter. Michelman agreed to that and Freeman left the hospital. A short time later, Michelman also left, saying he was going to meet with a judge.

"About twenty minutes later, he [Michelman] showed up and said he had been given the OK," the hospital official told the *Plain Dealer*. "I told him that seemed like a short time to get downtown and back."

Suspicious, the hospital administrator checked with the court and found out no permission had been given for the release of the child.

"I went down and talked to Michelman in the hospital emergency room," the administrator said, adding that the natural mother's family was upset because they believed the deal had already gone through and Michelman was to pay her hospital bill.

The administrator said he confronted Michelman, saying, "You told me you got permission and you didn't."

The lawyer reportedly responded, "Well, I certainly did."

The hospital official once again phoned Freeman and handed the telephone to Michelman. After his conversation, Michelman said that the court must have changed its mind.

The hospital refused to release the infant to either Michelman or his clients.

Later that day, the hospital official said he saw Michelman offering cash to a member of the natural mother's family. Court officials speculated the money was to be used for plane fare and expenses if a member of the family would fly the baby to New York.

It didn't work. That baby was later placed in the custody of the Lutheran Children's Society in Cleveland, which arranged for its adoption.

Another reason Michelman preferred to fly his clients to New York may have been a 1975 New York Attorney General's opinion that it was unlawful for New York lawyers to arrange private adoptions for babies born in another state. Michelman disagreed with this opinion, though, and claimed to have a way around it.

"It would be illegal for an attorney to go out of the state, take custody [of the baby], and bring it back in," he said. "It is not illegal for adoptive parents to go out of state, take custody, and proceed with the adoption here."

But it was easier still to bring the pregnant women to New York and avoid both the local problems of other states and the possible penalty if the Attorney General's opinion was correct.

Despite the profitability of his adoption business, Michelman apparently began getting nervous about both the amount of adverse publicity he was getting and increasing court scrutiny of his adoptions. Toward the end of 1976, he began passing the word that he was getting out of adoptions.

No one is sure for how long, however. In early 1977, a man representing himself as an attorney for Michelman & Michelman walked into the offices of the Child Welfare

League of America (CWLA), a New York-based social service agency that sets standards for adoption agencies throughout the country. This man allegedly said he was worried that the state was about to outlaw independent adoption and wanted to know whether the CWLA knew of any adoption-agency licenses for sale.

"It's as though he thought it was a liquor license," a League official said with undisguised disgust. "As though, with enough money, they could buy themselves into legitimacy."

Black market adoption's informal network of baby brokers survives and thrives through word-of-mouth referrals. Often a broker in one state supplies the baby and one in another state supplies the adoptive parents. By crossing state lines, both entrepreneurs are relatively safe from prosecution.

This network reaches into every state in the union, involving hundreds of baby brokers. Some handle several dozen adoptions each year; some only a few. But for all, babyselling is a highly profitable venture.

The natural mothers who supply the baby market are found in a variety of ways: through abortion counseling services; through referrals from other unwed mothers; through newspaper advertisements; through sources in foreign countries. Once in a great while, a woman actually sells her baby. More often, she is given little more than money for her living and medical expenses—about what she would be entitled to receive in a legitimate adoption. After all, anything that goes to the natural mother reduces the broker's profit, something he is unlikely to do willingly.

Potential customers are easier to find than are adoptable babies. Couples who want to adopt find the names of baby sources through friends, adoptive parents groups, relatives, attorneys, doctors, the news media. Often these couples will establish contact with the adoption entrepreneur themselves. Other times, a broker will initiate a meeting with a wealthy couple whose name he has obtained from similar sources.

These entrepreneurs are both shrewd and adaptable. When sources of American babies threatened to shrink, they supplied foreign babies. When the immigration authorities balked at letting these foreign children into the country, the baby brokers brought in pregnant women and had them give birth here. When some natural mothers changed their minds and wanted to keep their babies, the entrepreneurs invented worthless contracts for them to sign saying they agreed to repay everything spent on them if they kept their babies. When law enforcement officials became too interested in the black market there, the baby brokers learned to cross state lines to dilute those officials' authority.

With average prices for babies ranging as high as fifty thousand dollars and rising, annual profits in black market adoption total into the millions of dollars. If one thing is sure, with stakes that high and growing higher, and with little official opposition, the black market is going to expand further. Prices will rise and new sources of babies will be found and cultivated.

The baby brokers recognize easy money when they see it. They also recognize a low risk business. And they're going after both in the adoption black market.

CHAPTER FIVE

Why Doesn't Somebody
Do Something?

The people who are shocked by black-market adoptions and all the sleazy aspects of such transactions find it difficult to understand why nobody seems to be doing anything to stop it.

Indictments of babysellers are rare. Even more rare are convictions. To date, the only convictions are those of Ronald Silverton and Wayman Wilkes in Los Angeles. There are also current indictments in New Jersey and Washington, D.C., Suffolk County, New York, and in New York City. The fact that any cases can be cited at all is evidence that somewhat more is being done to stop the babysellers now than a few years ago. In spite of court actions, however, babyselling has grown and flourished, becoming a multi-million-dollar business.

The few indictments and arrests represent only a tiny tentative step toward the kind of law enforcement that could mean no child in this country will ever again become a piece of merchandise.

Why isn't more being done?

The answer to this question is complex and includes

legal impediments as well as the barrier of public apathy.

First of all, as any successful baby broker well knows, there is no uniform adoption law in the United States. There are fifty different states and fifty quite different laws. By its very nature, black-market adoption takes advantage of this situation. In almost every case, at least two, and often three, states will be involved in a transaction. This serves to create serious jurisdictional problems for officials trying to stop the babysellers.

Before a prosecutor of a black-market-adoption case can even begin unraveling the adoption laws of the various states involved, he or she must identify and locate the parties to that adoption—the baby broker, the natural mother, and the adoptive parents. That in itself may be nearly impossible. To make matters worse, adoption records in this country are sealed by court order to protect the identity of the people involved.

As an example, Los Angeles prosecutor Richard Moss said that, in the Ronald Silverton case, he would not have had names of adoptive parents and natural mothers involved in the Save-A-Life adoptions had Silverton not kept copies of court records in his personal files. Investigators, armed with a search warrant, seized those files. A prosecutor, however, cannot expect to be that lucky very often. And without the testimony of the adoptive parents and natural mother to support evidence that an adoption did take place and without information as to the circumstances surrounding that adoption, there is no case against the babyseller.

Donald Score, chief of the Operations Support Unit for the California State Department of Health, has investigated many babyselling complaints. He stresses that even after the parties to an adoption are identified and located they're hardly cooperative witnesses. "The natural mother is happy and doesn't want to talk about the experience because she doesn't want to be exposed as having had an illegitimate child. The adoptive parents are happy because they now have a child and it's apparently the quickest way—or the only way—they could get a child. And obviously the conduit [babyseller] who makes money on the transaction is not about to talk because he could get himself in terrible trouble."

Score's contention that all parties in the transaction are happy is not invariably true. In fact, the dissatisfaction of some natural mothers has led to quite a few babyselling investigations.

In New York City, for example, Assistant District Attorney Joseph Morello has been investigating black-market adoption for more than a year. He explained how one investigation was begun: "A young woman, a natural mother, gave up her child to a baby broker. She executed the necessary consents and all the other legal paperwork and then she wanted out. She, like most of these women, wasn't a New Yorker, but was from another state. Her attorney contacted our State Department of Social Services and they contacted us."

In that case, the natural mother was willing and eager to testify against the babyseller who had taken her child. She did not know, however, who the adoptive parents were since their identity was under seal in adoption records in their home state.

"That's marvelous in terms of protecting the privacy and sensitivities of everyone involved," Morello said, "but from the point of view of investigating a criminal transaction in an adoption those records may be vital evidence. That seal provision is a real stumbling block to investigation."

Courts across the country vary in their willingness to order those records opened for inspection. In New York one must get a court order to open the records, but at the same time notice is given the adoptive parents that such action has occurred. In other words, as soon as the court allows the investigator to see the records, the adoptive parents will be informed that such an inspection is taking place. This obviously puts the investigator at a distinct disadvantage. As Morello says, "Assuming they're involved in an illegal financial transaction, as soon as they get notice, they just tear up their bank records or whatever else. . . ."

Morello was asked to discuss the problems he has faced in trying to prosecute babyselling cases that cross state lines. His initial reaction was, "You got a week?" He chuckled as he said it, but the remark revealed some of the frustration inherent in his work.

Morello explained that, first of all, state lines mean distance and "distance means money."

"In a case we're now working on," he said, "the adoptive parents live in Florida, the natural mother is in Wisconsin, and the lawyer is in New York. Assuming we find out who all these people are (and this can be a pretty big assumption), the prosecutor has to get to Wisconsin and talk to whomever, and then go to Florida and talk to the other people. That means Morgenthau (the Manhattan District Attorney) has to pay for us to go there—two of us, usually, because New York police officers are not allowed to travel except two by two. So that's an obvious expense."

California's Donald Score also cited expense as a reason why more cases aren't prosecuted, and he put it into perspective for a smaller city.

"When you start talking about the amount of money

needed to prosecute such cases," he said, "given a flat budget for this district attorney's office, you're going to have to weigh the priorities.

"Say this thing is going to cost us X thousands of dollars to prosecute and we have X numbers of murders and rapes and high-visibility crimes. Then we have a D.A. saying, 'It's a good case and I like it, but we are not going to be able to get to it because we don't have the money.'

"In Los Angeles, they have a major fraud unit and they'd jump at a babyselling case. But let's say that same case happened in Madeira County, which has a low tax base. They'd say, 'Good lord, how can we handle this? We don't even have the money.' One case could wipe out their year's budget."

That expense can become prohibitive even for large cities like Los Angeles and New York. And the expense involved in sending investigators all over the country is only the beginning.

"The other end," Joseph Morello explained, "is that you've got to bring all these people here. So, even if the country was like one big state, these crimes would still be expensive to prosecute."

The United States, however, is not "one big state," and that brings in another problem Morello and other prosecutors have faced, that of jurisdiction.

"Our grand jury subpoena has legal force and effect only within the borders of this state," Morello said. "Similarly, a subpoena for a witness to attend has force only within this state."

So how does he persuade witnesses in Wisconsin and Florida to attend a grand jury proceeding in New York City? Isn't there cooperation between states in bringing witnesses before each other's grand juries?

Morello concedes that there is a national uniform act compelling the attendance of witnesses from another state in such a proceeding, but, he says, "No one ever uses it because it's a joke."

Luckily, the frustration level of Joseph Morello's job has not dampened his sense of humor.

"What it means basically is that a judge signs a subpoena for someone in, say, Santa Monica, California, to attend a trial here in New York. Then two police officers go to California where, dealing with either the state or county prosecutor, they go into Superior Court and make an application to that judge to enforce that subpoena. Then they go out and find the witness, take him, and bring him back to New York. Similarly, we could bring him back in custody if he were a material witness and we could have a warrant issued here for his arrest and then we'd go out to California and the Governor . . ." He breaks into laughter.

"You know," Morello said, "it's impossible to get a piece of paper moved in this court from one room to another. The amount of aggravation involved in bringing back a witness . . . I mean, look, if it was Carlo Gambino and what we needed was his secret recipe for some fantastic Italian food, then maybe we would do it—but nothing less than that."

He sums it up: "You could grow old waiting for an interstate subpoena enforcement."

The same jurisdictional problems that limit access to crucial witnesses also inhibit the ability to subpoena such vital elements as court records, bank records, and so on. A subpoena issued in one state has absolutely no authority in any of the other forty-nine. And you can bet your last dime that a smart baby broker will have made sure that the state in which he resides and transacts his business will not be the one in which the adoptive parents, the court adoption records, the parents' bank accounts, and so forth, are located.

For example, Morello said, "Let's say we want to find out about telephone calls, toll records. We know that a target (a babyseller) has been calling somebody in New Orleans, Louisiana, and we want to know who owns that phone. Now, in New York it's easy. We all know people in the phone company and they know we're bona fide, so we just send the letters and they say, 'All right, the subscriber is Jones.' But Louisiana will say, 'We don't know who you are. Get it from somebody else.' So every aspect of it is impossible."

Another kind of record vital to Morello's cases is hospital files. "We know that some of these baby lawyers enter into contracts with obstetricians to service the women and the obstetricians deliver these women at particular hospitals. After locating a number of these hospitals, needless to say, our next step is to subpoena their records.

"Now, in some instances, the hospital has been forthcoming and honored the grand-jury subpoena. In other instances, the hospital has decided that the privacy of these women is at stake and they've moved to quash the subpoena —so we may become involved in litigation over that."

Still another headache has been the fact that many— probably most—of the baby brokers are licensed attorneys. In some states, this may be enough to give them a legal shield for charging high fees. Florida's Walter Lebowitz can testify to that. The court there ruled he had the right to charge, literally, anything he wanted as a legal fee in an adoption.

Florida has since changed its law, but many other states still have that basic flaw.

Morello, though, is not worried about attorneys as defendants in the cases he is developing against New York baby brokers. Not yet. "The fact is," he said, "in this part of the country all the baby brokers are licensed attorneys, duly admitted, so if we're going to start worrying about that, we're going to stop prosecuting the case."

He outlined the strategy he planned to use before the grand jury: "What I'm trying to do is show that targets of my investigation are in the wholesale business of recruiting natural mothers on the one hand and, on the other, in the wholesale business of arranging adoptions. Therefore, I want to weave a carpet of facts which will make a lawyer's claim that the money he received was a legitimate legal fee ridiculous on its face.

"In addition to that, I'm hoping, ultimately, to be able to compare the sworn statements that the adoptive parents and their lawyer made in the adoption court proceedings to the adoptive parents' grand-jury testimony. I'm hoping that in their grand-jury testimony the adoptive parents will say, 'Yeah, I wrote that back then to secure the adoption, but that's not what it really was. What it really was is something else.'

"If I can get those two pieces together, no lawyer is going to be able to get up there and say, 'It really was a legal fee of ten thousand dollars and I just forgot to tell the court; I said it was twenty-five hundred.' I mean, at that point, it's conspiracy to commit perjury and obstruct justice, . . . and I'll rely on twelve good men and true to consign that particular story to the destiny to which it belongs."

The difficulty of convicting a babyseller doesn't begin and end with legal problems, however. A major hurdle is apathy on the part of the public and the courts.

Unfortunately—and bluntly—most people just don't see babyselling as a crime. Part of this attitude may stem from the traditional treatment of children as property. Society seems to tolerate a horrifying amount of child abuse, for example, because it thinks of a child as the "property" of its parents—and parents as having the right to discipline possessions, including children, as they please.

Is it so far from that attitude to believing it's acceptable to sell a child to someone else who is childless, particularly if the natural parent is willing to do so?

The most outspoken supporter of this kind of thinking is Phyllis Schlafly, the woman who has made a career out of opposing the Equal Rights Amendment. In 1977, she supported the decriminalization of babyselling, saying on her CBS radio show, "What's so wrong about that? If I hadn't been blessed with babies of my own, I would have been happy to have paid thousands of dollars for a baby."

While I hope not too many people agree with Mrs. Schlafly's stand, there certainly are great numbers who see babyselling as a victimless crime—something it definitely is not.

Joseph Morello admitted that, when he started investigating black-market adoption, he, too, thought of it as a victimless crime. He's since changed his mind.

He's found many people will say to him, "What's wrong with this? They're performing a public service, aren't they, the baby lawyers? Why do you want to waste your time on this?"

Morello has some well-thought-out answers. The baby lawyers are not, he says, performing a public service. They're in it for one reason: money. Then he proceeds to list the victims of this so-called victimless crime.

The first, and most important, victim is the child. "The law has mechanisms for establishing who is qualified to be a parent in an adoption situation," he said. "Everybody concedes that those mechanisms are not like the laws of physics, which have a high degree of accuracy in terms of their ability to predict success, but they are the mechanisms, and the only mechanisms available, and a three-day-old infant deserves to have those mechanisms invoked and applied.

"In a brokered baby situation, those mechanisms are going to be aborted. First of all, the original selection [of the adoptive parents] is not being made either by the natural mother or by an agency but by somebody who wants to know only the color of the adoptive parents' money. He doesn't give a damn whether these persons are incompetent in any way, as long as they are willing to pay.

"Then, the way the transaction is structured from that point on, everything possible is going to be done so that the courts draw a blank when they really try to look at the situation."

The second victim Morello cites is the natural mother. "With one sole exception," he said, "every natural mother we interviewed was a young girl in her teens who was faced with considerable embarrassment. These girls are beleaguered and frightened. By and large, they are not very bright—or at least not very sophisticated—and they have frequently fallen quite innocently into the hands of the baby broker. For example, a girl in Chicago reads an ad for an abortion counseling service, walks in the door and, the next thing she knows, somebody's trying to get her to sign legal papers. . . . She is completely unsophisticated about the meaning of the papers she, in fact, did sign.

"Then," Morello went on, "the baby lawyers and their staffs are going to cajole this girl about what a wonderful opportunity she's getting. Her baby is going into this great home. 'The father, who is a doctor, has won a Nobel Prize.

The mother is a Ph.D. They've got millions and the kid will have all the advantages, and what have you, whether it's true or not.

"So now the girl, without any independent counseling, is going to receive no legal advice.

"She tries to back out and they tell her, 'If you're going to back out now, you're going to have to pay for all this stuff that's happened already.'

"They put psychological pressure on her, telling her how her life as a bachelor mother will be a disaster or how she's breaking the hearts of this Nobel laureate and his wife.

"And ultimately she'll give up the baby.

"If a black-market baby broker has his way, nobody is ever going to sit down with this girl and talk to her about her real options."

Morello says the third possible victim is the adoptive parents, though Morello is not indulgent about them and their motivations. "From what I've been able to determine from the babyselling operations in this county," he said, "there's no way you could have enough wit to be able to earn the money to pay the baby brokers and not have enough wit to realize how sleazy this operation really is."

He does concede that the adoptive parents, even knowing what they have entered into, are often misled about the baby's health and heredity. "What do they do if the baby turns out not to be to their liking?" he asked. "I mean, they, too, have been sold a bill of goods—about the natural mother. 'Maybe she doesn't quite have a Ph.D.,' they're told, 'but she's on her way to getting one.' "

A fourth victim of black-market adoptions includes any number of would-be adoptive parents. "Let's start with a basic premise," Morello said. "First, all black-market babies are white children. All are, apparently, free of congenital defects. There are many more people who want to adopt these kids than there are kids to be adopted. Therefore there are waiting lists at agencies.

"You can assume that if Mr. and Mrs. Smith pay a baby broker ten thousand dollars to adopt Johnny, then Mr. and Mrs. Jones, who can't pay that fee but who are as competent as Mr. and Mrs. Smith, aren't going to get the baby. They may never get a baby. A fair shake of the dice might have put Johnny into their hands and provided them with the biggest thrill of their lives.

"They're not going to get the child . . . because they are unwilling to commit the crimes that are involved in this kind of transaction, or because they don't have the money."

Morello sees black-market adoption as, among other things, a crime against the poor. "Even assuming we're all willing to be perjurers and criminals, then this racket says, 'Here is the economic breakpoint. If you have more than that, we can start dealing, but if you don't, good-by, we don't want to talk to you.' "

The final victim of babyselling is the judicial system. "As a lawyer, two things bother me," Morello said. "Number one, the hoodwinking of the courts and, then, frankly, the fact that, until recently, the courts weren't doing a helluva lot to unhoodwink themselves. I agree that—if the courts really scrutinized these things—we could stop a lot of it, but it's a fact of life that they don't."

Over and over again during interviews for this book, the concern was expressed that the courts don't really care much about babyselling. The courts, too often, see their function in any kind of independent adoption as merely rubber-stamping applications. There was almost never any close scrutiny of parents, attorney, or child. Natural mothers, in a black-market situation, did not appear before the court in the final adoption proceeding. And one wondered if the social workers' home studies of the adoptive parents were even read by the judge, whose attitude seemed to be: This baby has been with these people for several months now and, whether the adoptive parents are good people or not, whether they purchased this baby or not, the child is better off staying with them than being moved to another environment. Witness the California case where the judge approved an adoption after the social worker had supplied him with proof that the adoptive parents had physically abused the infant.

Perhaps most eloquent on the subject of court apathy is Elizabeth Cole, director of the North American Center on Adoption:

"Not taking this seriously is a problem all through the black-market situation. Many judges think there's nothing wrong with this. 'This is a nice couple, so what? Maybe they paid a little money for the youngster, but they can afford it. They would have paid it for a vacation, or a trip around the world, or a house, but they'd like a child more, so what's the harm?' They just look the other way because they don't think it is a serious business.

"No matter what law you pass, you're going to have that problem. How are you going to overcome the attitude of the people who are supposed to enforce the law? I think that's where most attempts fall down: they think just by putting a law on the books, it's going to do the job, when, in fact, what they're really facing is an attitudinal problem."

Ms. Cole thinks there ought to be seminars held for officers of the court "where the chief judge impresses other judges with the seriousness of the problem, the fact that this is something they can't overlook."

Then, too, she said, "The agencies involved in investigations [home studies] ought to be able to bring appeals if they feel, in a particular case, the judge did not enforce the law.

"Somebody's got to monitor the performance of the court," she insisted. "The question is, who?"

After hearing a list of problems like the ones Joseph Morello is facing in his prosecutions, coupled with the apparent lack of concern on the part of the public and the courts, one begins to wonder if a prosecutor doesn't have to be a bit masochistic to even attempt to convict a baby broker. Why bother? In most of the cases that have been pursued in the courts, the reason has been a district attorney with a special interest in this type of crime.

In California, the late Los Angeles County District Attorney, Joseph P. Busch, had such an interest; it was his decision to prosecute Ronald Silverton *et al*. And in Manhattan, Joseph Morello said, "It's only because District Attorney Robert Morgenthau has a personal interest in prosecuting complex white-collar crime cases, and a personal interest in prosecuting this particular kind of crime, that we have had the time that these cases require. . . ."

There *are* solutions to the problem. Not easy ones, but solutions. Until the laws change and the courts and public become educated and concerned about the victims of black-market adoption, it will take courage, dedication, a high level of tolerance for frustration, and probably a few more concerned district attorneys before any progress can be made in stopping babyselling.

CHAPTER SIX

Should Private Adoption
Be Outlawed?

There are many adoption professionals, particularly those working for agencies, who think there is a simple solution to stopping black-market adoption: outlaw all independent placements. Give the business to agencies exclusively and black-market adoption cannot exist, the theory goes.

This is the policy of Joseph Reid and the Child Welfare League of America. The League, established in 1920, is a national, voluntary organization providing service to the child-welfare field. It accredits adoption agencies and sets standards for them. Its membership totals some four hundred agencies in the fifty states and Canada.

Reid has, with good reason, been outspoken against the travesty of black-market adoptions. He feels that if there were no independent adoptions at all, the black market would die. He would like to see the day when all adoptions go through agencies.

But that solution to the problem of babyselling may be too simplistic. It has three major drawbacks: lack of proof that adoption agencies really do a significantly better job of placing children than do ethical attorneys and physicians; certain human rights of the natural mothers would be abridged if private placement were outlawed; and, finally, prohibiting independent adoptions could force the black market into another, more deeply hidden, form that would be even worse for the children involved.

To date, four states—Connecticut, Delaware, Minnesota, and Michigan—have outlawed independent adoptions between non-relatives. The other forty-six permit private adoptions with varying restrictions.

Vehemently arguing against the Child Welfare League's stand to abolish independent adoption is Beverly Hills, California, attorney David Leavitt, who has handled more than eight hundred private adoptions over a seventeen-year period and admits that approximately ninety-five percent of his law practice involves the adoption or custody of children, juvenile court matters, guardianships, and other things having to do with the rights and custody of children.

Leavitt's charge for an adoption is eight hundred and fifty dollars, plus an additional three hundred and fifty if special procedures have to be used to terminate the rights of the unwed father. His legal fees are the same whether he finds the baby or the adoptive parents find it on their own.

David Leavitt is one of the most successful gray-market adoption lawyers in the country. He is an ethical adoption attorney, as well as a man who sees his own status threatened by the black-market entrepreneurs' excesses. In his home state he has been outspoken against people like Ronald Silverton because he fears that publicity surrounding high-profit adoption lawyers may force legislation outlawing all private adoptions. Leavitt argues that an experienced, ethical attorney or physician can do at least as good a job of arranging an adoption as can a social worker in an agency.

"The idea that a lawyer interested in this field cannot become every bit as expert as some social worker is ridiculous," he said. "I think, generally speaking, we've got a lot smarter bunch of people in the law schools than we have in the social-work schools. And God knows we have three times as much training and we go through a lot more to get our licenses than social workers do." In some areas, Leavitt claims, attorneys actually do a better job of arranging adoptions than do social workers. He also claims that agencies often can inhibit adoptions.

Leavitt likes to substantiate his opinions with statistics and, while an intelligent person can make statistics say almost anything, some of his numbers are quite persuasive.

The first statistic Leavitt offers is that eighty percent of pregnant girls who approach an agency keep their babies rather than give them up for adoption. Of the girls who come to him, he says, the numbers are reversed; about ninety-five percent of his group release their babies for adoption. Some observers would say that this fact is further proof that adoption attorneys tend to coerce unwed mothers into giving up their babies while agencies present them with all possible alternatives, but Leavitt disagrees. "I think many adoption-agency workers consider it their duty to talk a girl out of an adoption." Their attitude, he said, is that "a girl who is pregnant out of wedlock and considers adoption is psychologically diseased. So, obviously, you can't treat her like a rational adult, a thinking, intelligent person.

"If you were pregnant out of wedlock," he went on, "and you went into an agency, and you were faced with a social worker who started looking down her nose at you, as if your thinking was a little funny, you just might believe her. If you resented what she said and didn't believe her, then your belief in her expertise would go down the tube. If you couldn't believe in her expertise, how in the world could you believe in that agency's expertise to give away your baby?"

Leavitt is, perhaps, too hard on agency personnel. A good percentage of the unwed mothers-to-be may approach an adoption agency in order to learn more about alternative solutions to their problem, not because they have decided they definitely want an adoption.

His argument does have some ring of truth to it, however.

When Lynne McTaggart of the *New York Daily News* was researching her article on the black market, she visited several New York City adoption agencies, posing as an unwed mother seeking an adoption. Her experiences with these agencies were not encouraging. At one, she said, "It took me most of the first visit to convince her [the social worker] that I did *not* want foster care for the child or an abortion."

Surely most agency workers try hard to present all available options to the pregnant girls who approach them. Perhaps, in their ardor, they try so hard *not* to unduly push adoption that they give the impression that, with the various kinds of welfare available to her, a girl would be foolish to give up her baby.

Whatever his reason for using them, Leavitt's statistics in this instance are right. Joseph Reid concurs that, indeed, eighty percent of the pregnant girls who approach agencies for adoption information do keep their babies. This may be good for those women able to support and love their babies, but what about the thirteen- and fourteen-year-olds who are really children themselves? A horrifying number of these adolescent mothers actually think their babies are either live toys or someone who will love them as their own parents never did. Of course an infant is neither a toy nor an unselfish lover. The predictable result is two young lives ruined—the girl's because she drops out of school with no marketable skills and finds herself destined to a life on welfare; and the baby's, because no child can possibly be what a child-mother wants it to be. The baby ends up being resented and, too often, abused and neglected. Some social workers say they are now seeing some of these babies relinquished for adoption—but not until they are two or three years old and their teen-age mothers have tired of the parenthood game. These toddlers are, by that time, psychologically disturbed, bearing scars that can never be erased.

While our society cannot force a mother to give up her child and still pretend to be a free society, surely the hazards of a young girl's keeping her infant should be stressed to her, both for her own benefit and her baby's.

If agencies hinder adoptions, well-intentioned state laws do the same. Leavitt thinks that as a result of these state laws, black-market adoptions will only increase. As an example he cites Connecticut, which changed its law to prohibit independent adoptions in 1960. In 1959, there were 1092 adoptions in Connecticut, of which fifty-eight percent were private placements. In 1960, as soon as a new law governing adoption went into effect, ninety-six percent of all adoptions were agency placements, but there were only 573 placements made, a decline of almost half in one year's time. Further, Leavitt says, in 1973, there were only 126 adoptions in Connecticut, a ninety-percent drop since 1959. Over the same period of time, the number of adoptions in his own state of California remained about the same.

What happened to Connecticut? There may be a variety of reasons for the decrease in children adopted, but surely the prohibition of independent adoptions has to be largely responsible for a drop of fifty percent in one year.

Since there was no particular nationwide shortage of adoptable babies in 1960, it would seem that Leavitt's argument has some merit.

He also likes to cite figures comparing numbers of adoptions in states that encourage independent adoption to numbers in those states prohibiting or discouraging such adoptions.

His figures for 1973, taken from a national survey by Opportunity, a division of the Boys and Girls Aid Society of Oregon, show a great gap among certain states. For example, of states that encourage independent adoption, Iowa had 45.2 adoptions per 100,000 population, Utah had 45.1, and California had 28.6. Of states that make private adoption fairly difficult, New York had only 11 adoptions per 100,000 population, New Jersey had 10.2, and Colorado had 4.3. Two states, Delaware and Connecticut, which have outlawed private adoption altogether, had 4.5 and 4.2 adoptions per 100,000 population, respectively.

Again, there seems to be evidence that making adoption more difficult—*i.e.,* either outlawing or discouraging independent adoption—tends to reduce the total number of adoptions.

Another argument against giving adoption agencies a monopoly is that some of them have been known to be as corrupt and inefficient in their own ways as have any adoption attorneys.

In the 1950s a committee chaired by the late Senator Estes Kefauver found evidence that agencies in Illinois and Tennessee were selling babies. And, in 1973, the California State Assembly heard testimony that a Nevada adoption agency was requiring a substantial "contribution" before it would place a child with a couple. Though these shocking incidents are rare, a common criticism of adoption agencies is that some social workers, who know they have great power over people—the power to relieve them of their childlessness—like to "play God" with applicants. There have been numerous reports that agencies have inquired into couples' sexual habits to an extent which can hardly be necessary, and other reports of social workers trying to trick applicants. Some, it seems, enjoy seeing couples squirm trying to deal with unanswerable questions. For example, sometimes a husband is told, "Your wife wants to adopt more than you do. What do you think of that?" There is no way such a question can be answered correctly. It's really akin to the classic, "When did you stop beating your wife?"

One Pennsylvania woman was told by an adoption agency to quit both her college classes and her job so she could sit home to wait for a baby. "They told me, 'Look, if you're in school when the baby comes, you're not getting it.' So I quit school. Then they made me quit my job too."

Although the agency told the woman that she had to be home all day before they would place a baby with her, they refused to give her an estimated time when a child might be available. As a result, the woman needlessly lost a full semester of school—not to mention five months of income.

A Catholic agency in the East is notorious for asking applicants their position on birth control. If they say they favor it under any circumstances, they do not get a baby from that agency. Now, the logic of making an infertile couple toe the Church line on birth control is odd to say the least. But applicants to that agency must simply learn to lie if they don't agree with the agency's "correct" answer.

One couple was told by a Protestant agency that they couldn't have a baby because they didn't attend a church. They were not churchgoers on principle—they didn't believe in organized religion—but that didn't matter to the agency.

The couple was told to join a church or forget about a child. They joined, but did they become better parental risks after having compromised their principles to get a baby?

Another woman was told she couldn't adopt because she was more than ten pounds overweight. She'd been overweight all her life, but dieted and managed to lose the excess pounds. Once her baby was adopted, of course, the weight went right back on.

Agencies have the power to force people to suffer almost any indignity. "They have you coming and going," one adoptive parent said, "because it's not something you want but you'll get over. You don't ever get over wanting a kid."

Robert Monsour, a New York attorney who handled adoptions until the baby shortage became acute, is also an adoptive father. According to him, agency adoptions have always been difficult in his state, even before the baby shortage, "because of their own requirements, not because of the scarcity of children."

One of the most important of these requirements was religious background of the prospective adoptive parents. In order for a Jewish couple to adopt, for example, they had to find a "Jewish baby." In reality, there are almost never any Jewish babies available for adoption. The result was a near prohibition against Jewish couples adopting. Even more difficult was an adoption by a couple with mixed religions. They had no place to go.

Another common problem with New York agencies, Monsour said, was that couples had to medically substantiate that they could not conceive a child. "In many, many cases—I'd say the majority of the cases I've handled and even in my own personal instance—inability to conceive was due to an emotional problem. It had nothing to do with fertility. As a result of that, the agencies would not give you a child. You had to go through every gynecological test known before you could satisfy them that you couldn't conceive."

Needless to say, many couples who have dealt with adoption agencies have come away completely demoralized. A probable outcome of an agency monopoly in adoptions would be not only to further diminish the number of babies available for adoption, but to inhibit thousands of couples from the hope of adopting as well. Among these would be Jewish couples; mixed religion couples; couples who practice no religion; couples with one member, or both, over the age of thirty-five; couples who cannot medically document infertility; couples who have one or more natural or adopted children; and so on. These are just a few of the types of families adoption agencies have traditionally found unsuitable. In a time of shortage, there would be no incentive to change these rigid requirements.

Adoption agencies are not without their own financial motives, either. Sharon Horner of Philadelphia's Adoptive Parents Group put it succinctly: "Even with agencies, what you can pay counts. They may have a sliding scale, but then they'll look at two couples and say, 'This is a great couple here, but their place on the scale is going to be five hundred dollars and this other couple is just as good and their scale is three thousand dollars.' They're going to go with the couple who can pay the higher fee. They need the money. Even the agencies have a profit motive."

Another, even more questionable, practice by agencies was cited by Robert Monsour. He claimed that agencies have a financial incentive (at least in his state) not to have the baby adopted at all.

"If the mothers give up the baby, the agencies generally place it into foster care, and that can last for the child's whole minority. They do this because, in foster care, the agency receives X number of dollars a year from the state. The agencies take their expenses off the top and remit the balance to the foster parents. The practice is, in essence, funding the agencies. They would put themselves out of business if they placed all the children for adoption."

Monsour's contention was partially contested by Elizabeth Cole of the North American Center on Adoption. "What the lawyers are telling you is true," she said, "except that it doesn't apply to the children they're talking about." Ms. Cole said that an agency today would always place a healthy white infant for adoption. "As a matter of fact," she said, "the City of New York pays the adoption agency a fee of $1795 to cover the costs of every child that's placed for adoption, so there is incentive for agencies to place babies."

Ms. Cole does admit, however, that placing children in foster homes, instead of finding adoptive parents, has been prevalent for babies and children who are considered hard to place. "It's true that there are financial incentives to the agency not to place handicapped youngsters, older children, black children, children who've been in foster care for several years," she said.

But the financial incentives are only part of the problem. An even bigger difficulty is that social workers simply don't believe this type of child can be placed, they don't understand that there are couples who would want to adopt it, so they don't even try.

Ms. Cole's contention that black-market adoption deals only with healthy infants, usually white, is substantially correct, but some couples waiting for a child would surely adopt an older, handicapped, or minority-race child if one were available. Especially since the time seems to have passed when even these children are readily available to would-be parents.

For example, when Sharon Horner wanted to adopt her third child, she applied to a full dozen adoption agencies. She was willing to take any child, under the age of five, except one who was mentally handicapped. A child of any race with almost any physical handicap would have suited the Horners. Even so, it took them more than three years to get a child, a toddler from Korea who will someday need expensive corrective surgery.

Though Mrs. Horner is delighted with her new daughter, she still feels it's a shame that they couldn't have found an American child somewhere—one who was being shuffled among foster homes—to add to their family.

Licensing requirements for adoption agencies vary greatly from state to state. While one state's requirements might be quite strict, resulting in fully trained and qualified persons arranging placements, others are less rigid. Illinois, for example, does not even require that an adoption agency be operated as a non-profit organization.

And, once a group or person has a license in one state—even a state with loose requirements—it becomes relatively easy to expand into other states.

Elizabeth Cole illustrated: "Once you become licensed in State A and you can put on your letterhead that you're a licensed agency, most states have reciprocity. If you're licensed in State A and you want to place a baby in State B, they'll say, 'Well, you must be legitimate if you're licensed in State A. Go ahead.' Some states are a little fussier, but that's the exception, not the rule. And some of the licensing laws in some of the states are so poor . . ."

Obviously, merely having a license to place children for adoption does not always mean that those placements will be successful, ethical, or even non-profit.

Another reason it would be unwise to prohibit all private adoption is that this would mean a natural mother would no longer have the right to find a home for her child herself. She would have to relinquish that task to organizations with whose principles she may disagree. In most states today a pregnant woman retains the right to place her baby with people she knows and trusts. In the four states prohibiting private adoption, she can no longer do that. In those states, she has lost a basic human right. She cannot go to a trusted family physician or attorney for help in finding an adoptive home for her child either. It seems logical that, in certain circumstances, a woman or girl might feel much more confident about a decision to have her child adopted if she knows the family has been selected by someone with whom she is familiar, someone she trusts.

Additionally, in many private adoptions, a mother has the right to know where her baby will be placed if both she and the adoptive parents agree to this arrangement. If she were forced to go through an agency, she would no longer have that right.

Many people think it dangerous for a natural mother to know which family has adopted her baby, and would recommend that information be withheld from her. David Leavitt, however, says this fear is both groundless and ridiculous.

"It shocks people throughout the United States," he said, "that in California these cases are open. But why shouldn't they be? If you go on the folklore basis that a girl who has a baby she's thinking of putting up for adoption is crazy, then all these things—secrecy, cloak-and-dagger—make sense. But only in the context that she is really a crazy girl.

"If, on the other hand, you think of her as a rational girl who needs that adoption as much as those adopting parents, then all this folklore seems ridiculous—and it *is* ridiculous. Without that adoption, that girl's future is knocked into a cocked hat. She can't take responsibility for her baby. By coming along, that adopting couple is saving her life, just as she is saving them from a childless existence. You've got to realize that this is a two-way street being traveled by rational people."

Leavitt's personal experience reinforces his contentions. "Out of eight-hundred and fifty adoptions I've had five infants returned [to their natural mothers] in seventeen years," he said. "In not one of those five cases did the natural and adoptive parents meet one another. I have never had a child returned where the natural and adoptive parents have met." And, in many, many of the Leavitt adoptions, the natural and adoptive parents do meet.

Enforcing a ban on private adoption is certainly treading on the basic rights of the natural mother. In addition, it seems logical that, when a girl who wants to know the family that will raise her baby, or who wants to choose adoptive parents she herself trusts, or who wants her family doctor or lawyer to help her choose such a couple, is told she cannot do any of these things, she is likely to keep her baby rather than release it for adoption.

The final and most persuasive argument against forbidding private adoption is that it just doesn't do what it is intended to do: stop babyselling. In fact, it might even raise the prices on the black market. The going price of babies, after all, is regulated by supply and demand. The demand is not going to go away, but outlawing private adoption will reduce the supply of babies.

The way the black market works in the states that have already outlawed private adoption is totally devastating for the child. Even more so than in the other forty-six states. Where independent adoption is illegal, many couples simply add a child obtained through the black market to their family. Since the child is never actually adopted, he has no legal status.

Elizabeth Cole said her personal feeling about banning private adoption differs from the Child Welfare League of America's official stand, even though the North American Center on Adoption, which she directs, is a branch of the League.

"What really bothers me about outlawing independent adoption," she said, "is that it's the kids who suffer most from that solution. You're never really going to stop people who want to have children and can't get them. They can't give birth to them and they can't get them through regular adoption channels. The situation is going to remain the same—more people wanting more babies than there are available. So the people who want babies are going to find them. They're going to find them anyplace they can."

Ms. Cole has observed that in the four states that outlaw private adoption, people still get black-market babies. They just run into more harmful problems for the child.

"What happens," she said, "is that couples get the babies, and take them home. These laws [outlawing non-agency adoptions] then prohibit the couple from going into court and legally adopting these children.

"Now they've got their babies and they're raising them, but the children don't have any legal parents, they don't have any rights of inheritance. Their custody is cloudy if anybody really wants to make a fuss over it. So the person who suffers the most from a prohibition against independent adoption is the youngster."

Ms. Cole said she has asked officials in the states now outlawing private adoption what happens when they find a good family who has an "illegal" child in their home. "I was told," she said, "that the family has several recourses. They can go down to court and legally have that child's name changed to the family's, or the adoptive family is prohibited from going into court to adopt the child, but can ask to be made the legal guardian of that child.

"So my question was, 'Then what's the effect of the prohibition?' It's a charade in a sense. The other thing that happens is a lot of couples will wait until the child is eighteen and then it doesn't matter—they can go into court and adopt him after he becomes an adult under a different provision of the adoption laws."

The result of this prohibition is, then, that families keep the child, but live in constant fear of exposure to the authorities. They obtain forged birth certificates, when the child starts school. If the parents die, the child's situation is revealed and he becomes a ward of the state and goes into a foster home instead of being sent to "relatives," since legally he has none. The main result is a life of uncertainty, fear, and surreptitiousness for both the child and its would-be parents.

Ruth Weidell, Adoption Supervisor for the Minnesota Welfare Department, explained what happens to a family in that state who obtains a baby from an illegal source (*i.e.*, other than a licensed adoption agency). She illustrated her explanation with two cases of families who had paid large sums of money for out-of-state babies and then tried to get a Minnesota adoption. Legally, Ms. Weidell said, the child should be returned to the state in which it was born (the sending state).

In the first case she cited, Ms. Weidell's department informed the sending state of the situation. Minnesota and the sending state recommended that a court order be obtained to have the baby removed from the prospective adoptive home and returned. In that instance, though, Ms. Weidell said, "A lot of politics were involved," with various officials refusing to be the first to act. As a result of this inaction, the child remained in the home and an adoption eventually took place.

The second family was less lucky. They brought their baby into Minnesota when it was just a few days old and attempted to adopt it. In a complicated series of court orders and legal maneuvers, the baby was first placed in a foster home in Minnesota for a few months, and then transferred to a foster home in the sending state. Guardianship was eventually assigned to a licensed adoption agency in the sending state. That agency, according to Ms. Weidell, "very generously selected the original Minnesota family, so we then brought the child back into the state . . . and made an agency placement."

The family who had wanted to adopt that baby and had "paid" for that privilege did ultimately adopt it, but not until the child was about six months old and had lived in three different homes. Surely that kind of process cannot be healthy for the child involved.

Other families in Minnesota have simply moved to another state if adoption officials started investigating their questionable situations too closely, thereby ensuring they wouldn't lose their child.

And, of course, Ms. Weidell and the Minnesota Welfare Department find out about only those situations in which a family naively tries to adopt a child despite the state law or in which someone reports the fact that a family has an unrelated child in its home. This likely represents only a minuscule portion of the illegal situations in the state.

For many reasons, independent adoption should not be banned as a proposed cure for the black market. There is no concrete evidence that agencies do a better job of placing children than do ethical attorneys and physicians, and it's obvious that abolishing private placements unfairly restricts the natural mothers' rights. Additionally, figures show that an agency monopoly would further reduce the number of babies available for adoption. Most important, an agency monopoly would not stop babyselling. It would only make those involved go further underground, resulting in an even more harmful situation for the children involved. It would also increase the price being asked for babies since the supply would decrease while the risk of those involved increases. Basically, a prohibition on private adoption would cause more problems than it would solve.

But there are some logical solutions to black-market adoptions. They just aren't simple.

CHAPTER SEVEN

Solutions

A variety of solutions has been proposed to curb babyselling. One, prohibition of all private adoptions, has, as just documented, inherent difficulties. Other solutions seem more likely to be successful in helping to eradicate this problem.

An attempt to solve some of the problems relating to the transportation of children across state lines for the purpose of adoption has been outlined in the Interstate Compact on the Placement of Children. The first signatory to this Compact was New York, in 1960. By 1977, forty-one states had signed. The bill is, however, a partial, not a complete, solution to some of the problems of interstate adoptions, although some interested persons, such as David Leavitt, would disagree.

The Compact does have some excellent provisions. Under its rules, a child cannot be brought into a receiving state until written notice is given that state by the sending state of who the natural parent and prospective adoptive parents are, and the reasons for the necessity of an interstate adoption. The Compact administrator in the receiving state must then approve the child's transfer. Before he issues that approval, however, the prospective adoptive parents must undergo a home study to determine their suitability as parents. The Compact, then, in cooperating jurisdictions, establishes a record-keeping system and determines parental suitability *before* a child is permitted to enter the receiving state—a major step forward.

Brendan Callanan, Project Director for the Compact, which is a creation of the American Public Welfare Association of Washington, D.C., thinks the Compact has already helped to cut down on black-market adoptions in the forty-one signatory states. "What the Compact did was to say that a violation of the laws of one signatory state was a violation of both states' laws and could be prosecuted in either state or both states."

Callanan said he's had a number of calls from attorneys concerned about whether or not they have to follow the Compact. They know full well that if they ignore it and one state gets upset at them and both of the states are in the Compact—they can be reached.

Difficulties arise, however, that inhibit the Compact's effectiveness. First, all fifty states are not signatories. Those states which, as of August, 1977, had not yet adopted the Compact were Nevada, Alabama, South Carolina, Arkansas, New Jersey, Wisconsin, Michigan, Hawaii, and Indiana. Some of those states were, at that time, considering signing.

Another problem with the Compact is that it has to rely on state laws for penalties. These can range from a small fine, to loss of a license, to several years in prison. As Joseph Reid of the Child Welfare League of America said, "The Interstate Compact on the Placement of Children depends wholly on state laws. If you have states with weak laws, having a Compact does not necessarily help that situation. If you have two states with very weak laws [involved in one particular transaction], it is very bad. We have had states, and do have states, that are centers for this type of activity [babyselling]."

Elizabeth Cole noted additional problems with the Compact: "Crooks aren't going to abide by it. If somebody doesn't tell the Interstate Compact Administrator that they're bringing a baby into the state for black-market purposes, the Administrator isn't going to be able to do anything about it."

Ms. Cole also said, "Another deficit is that the courts haven't been tuned in. Some of the judges don't even know there is something called the Interstate Compact. When a lawyer brings a case with an out-of-state baby into court here in New York, the judge doesn't routinely ask, 'Did you go through the Interstate Compact?' And even if he did ask, what's the sanction? What happens to you if you don't go through the Compact? The law says you lose your license to place children, but the entrepreneur doesn't have a license to place children. What's he going to lose? An agency would lose its license, but not an entrepreneur.

"Some people have interpreted the statute to mean that the attorney involved can lose his license to practice law," Ms. Cole continued. "Yes, technically, but do you really think that's going to happen when the courts don't think there's anything really wrong and don't even ask if there's an Interstate Compact?"

And what if the babyseller is not an attorney? Then what does he stand to lose?

Callanan agreed there is not enough judicial awareness of the Compact, but it is something he's working on. "We've met with the National Council of Juvenile Court Judges, headquartered in Reno, Nevada, and have decided to join with them to institute training programs for the judges who come into their college, which provides continuing education programs. We hope to get into the 1978 curriculum and bring a new awareness of the Compact to the judges attending." Callanan hopes that eventually all judges working with adoptions will be fully cognizant of the Compact's provisions. "The idea is that the judges who attend these training programs will return to their individual states and assume responsibility for putting on state-level training sessions."

In addition to stimulating greater court awareness of the Compact and its provisions, Ms. Cole suggested another way to make the agreement stronger than it now is: change the court rules and regulations to order the judge to ask—in every case—whether or not this adoption has gone through the Compact administrator, and then keep a record of the attorney's answer.

"In this manner if attorney Jones goes into court the first time and says, 'Gee, Your Honor, I didn't know it existed,' the judge may say, 'Okay, this time you get off, but you ought to know about it.' Then, the next time attorney Jones went into court, he couldn't use the same excuse.

"But," Ms. Cole says, "there's got to be some teeth in the enforcement of the Compact. If you don't go through the Compact administrator, the judge has got to do something more than swat you on the wrist and say, 'Next time be a good boy.' And the Interstate Compact just doesn't provide any penalties and sanctions."

Brendan Callanan explained that the penalties attached to violation of the Compact are contained in the laws of each state that has adopted it. "The code of each state has a certain section devoted to child-welfare activities," he said, "and if you violate their placement statute, there's another section of the code that specifies the penalty. The Compact is just one of the placement statutes. It would be chaos if each of the provisions had its own penalty; it'd be terribly unwieldy. So what we have to do is accept the state's own penalty statute."

Los Angeles County Assistant District Attorney Moss added several more deficiencies he sees in the Compact. At the core "there is no prohibition against profit-motivated organizations engaging in adoption activity. There are no provisions to check, control, or eliminate the amount or character of finders' fees, referral charges, or adoption costs. And, finally, there is no disclosure requirement that all direct or indirect costs, fees, and charges requested, paid or agreed upon, be revealed in any of the specified documentation."

When the Compact does not even attempt to deal with the essentials of babyselling—the exchange of money for a child—it certainly cannot hope to prevent the activity.

It seems that the real solution to babyselling cannot come from just one source. It has to come from a combination of sources—federal and state legislation and a commitment by the courts to enforce that legislation.

Missing now is federal legislation to prohibit the interstate transportation of children, including unborn children, for profit in adoptions or other permanent care arrangements. There are comprehensive federal laws regulating the interstate transport of everything from laboratory research animals to exotic birds. Can there be less for children?

A federal law to prohibit babyselling would not mean that the federal government would regulate adoptions. None of the existing state powers need be removed. It would simply become a crime to transport a child from one state to another for the purpose of placing that child—for money—

into any kind of permanent care. Such a law should also make it a crime to coerce, entice, or cajole a natural mother to give up her baby for such an adoption.*

There are many reasons why federal law is needed. As Richard Moss said, "The very character of these adoptions depends on the interstate transportation of children." Manhattan's Assistant District Attorney Morello also supports legislation at the federal level.

"These are going to be difficult crimes to prosecute whether there's federal legislation or whether there isn't," he said, "but the United States Attorney and the Department of Justice have certain intrinsic advantages. First, they have the money, which is an advantage the federal government always has over local law enforcement agencies. Second, they have manpower to burn in the FBI. Third, they have the jurisdiction—a subpoena from a United States district office is good throughout the country.

"Also," Morello continued, "there are certain evidentiary rules that apply in the federal system that do not apply in New York [or many other states]. For example, in New York you cannot put hearsay evidence before a grand jury; you must have direct evidence. Grand-jury investigations in New York are really mini-trials. But a federal grand jury may take hearsay evidence. So, at that level, you can have an agent come into a federal grand jury and say, 'On April first, I was in Miami and spoke with Miss Smith and she informed me that she had a baby. She told me she received one thousand dollars from Lawyer Jones and gave him the baby in the southern district of New York on such and such a day. . . .' That's sufficient evidence to indict

* The United States Senate has recently passed just such a law prohibiting the interstate transportation of young boys for the purpose of prostitution.

him and the government doesn't even have to bring these people into the southern district." In a New York investigation, Miss Smith would have to be brought from Miami to testify in person.

"Still another advantage of the federal government, is the conspiracy statute. They don't have to have corroboration for their conspirators. We do. We must have extra evidence because all co-conspirators are accomplices and therefore you need a little extra evidence to convict. Then, too, federal convictions stand up better."

Morello also pointed out that the federal government has certain investigative resources that could be put to use at the instigation of a local prosecutor if federal law pertaining to this kind of crime existed.

"Right now," he said, "if we asked the FBI to check on a piece of evidence in Terre Haute, Indiana, they would say they have no jurisdiction and ask to be shown the federal statute that allows them to do it.

"Other services, such as the State Department, or the Immigration and Naturalization Service, which could be of great use in some of the international aspects of these cases, . . . have to be able to account for their time. So they'd better be working on something that has to do with Uncle Sam," Morello concluded.

Virtually every prosecutor interviewed in relation to babyselling supports federal legislation to prohibit this crime. Without it, the battle simply cannot be won.

Several bills to prohibit babyselling have been introduced in Congress over the last twenty or more years, but none of them has become law.

The first congressional action was introduced by the late Senator Estes Kefauver, of Tennessee, in 1956. His bill would have made it a crime to transport a child across state lines for adoption-at-a-profit and would have made the coercion or enticement of a woman to give up her baby for such an adoption a crime as well. A third provision of the Kefauver bill made it illegal for a child to be transported across state lines for purposes of permanent care unless an investigation had first been made, by the public department responsible for child welfare in the receiving state, into both the circumstances surrounding the adoption and the suitability of the prospective adoptive family. This provision was to be waived if the placement were made by a licensed child-care or adoption agency or by the natural parent herself without the assistance of a third party. The provision was similar to the one now included in the Interstate Compact. The Kefauver statute, had it been enacted, would have applied to all fifty states, and eliminated the difficulty of having each state ratify such a bill independently.

By 1965, the Kefauver bill had been refined and was re-introduced in the Senate by Senator Dodd of Connecticut, who said he "picked it up" after Kefauver's death. Dodd told the Senate, "This measure was long championed by our late distinguished colleague, Senator Kefauver of Tennessee. He always encouraged me to press on with it. All the ground-work and spadework was done by him.

"Subsequently, due to the interest generated by Senator Kefauver, through the years the bill has been scrutinized, refined, and endorsed by the cooperative efforts of many skilled and knowledgeable persons, both in the Senate and in other governmental departments, concerned with the welfare of the children of this nation. . . . This bill would not infringe upon state laws or responsibilities; it would not abolish private or non-agency adoptions; it would not abolish interstate or foreign adoptions; it would not deprive parents of the right to seek new homes for their children without agency intervention; it would not prevent childless couples from seeking to adopt a child directly from its natural mother; and it would not prohibit receipt of professional fees for adoption-connected legal or medical services, childbirth, prenatal or postnatal care and the adoption proceeding itself. Any fear that it would delimit private adoptions and force everyone to rely on agencies is groundless."

In other words, the bill was intended to do one thing and only one thing—stop babyselling. It placed no unreasonable limits on anyone involved in adoption on an ethical, nonprofit basis.

In 1965, the bill passed the Senate. The House, however, adjourned before voting on it, and the bill subsequently died.

In 1975, extensive hearings to determine the scope of black-market adoption were held by the Senate Subcommittee on Children and Youth, chaired by now-Vice President Walter Mondale, but no bills to stop babyselling ever came out of those hearings.

In 1977, two bills were introduced, one in the Senate by Harrison Williams of New Jersey and one in the House, by Representative Henry Hyde of Illinois. Though both seek, once again, to outlaw babyselling without prohibiting any legitimate adoptions, neither provides for a preplacement investigation of the adoptive family or circumstances surrounding the adoption, as the Kefauver bill did. This essential requirement could be handled on a state level as well as on a federal level, or by the Interstate Compact, if ratified by all fifty states.

The Williams bill is the superior because it contains a proviso referring to transportation of the in utero child in interstate and foreign commerce. The Hyde bill, on the other hand, simply ignores the common practice of transporting the pregnant woman rather than waiting until her child is born and transporting the child.

Williams' staff feels confident his bill will receive full consideration in the near future (the bill is now before the Senate Judiciary Committee).

But the legal process is a slow one. And it has seldom been slower than in its attempts to outlaw black market adoption. There have been congressmen interested in stopping the traffic in babies for more than twenty years and still no law has been passed. Why?

Joseph Reid was asked by Walter Mondale at the 1975 hearings why the Kefauver-Dodd bill had not passed ten years earlier. He replied, "There are several reasons. . . . One was that careful work with the American Bar Association and the American Medical Association had not preceded this legislation. There were many lawyers, particularly those in small towns, [for whom] handling a few adoptions a year was a perfectly legitimate part of their practice, and who were not selling babies but were simply acting as an intermediary without fault or profit. . . . The same is true of doctors. . . . I think—well—there was just not enough understanding of what was involved. . . . And there was a lot of hostility toward adoption agencies."

In other words, the bill did not become law because people were afraid it would do just those things Senator Dodd said it would *not* do—prohibit private adoption, force people to go to agencies, stop lawyers and doctors from collecting legitimate fees, et cetera.

That kind of misinformation continues today. Additionally, there are two other reasons legislation has not passed—a general apathy in Congress and the public about babyselling; and a definite reluctance on the part of the legislators, many of whom are attorneys themselves, to pass bills limiting the legal profession in any way.

At a recent meeting of the House Judiciary Committee that was hearing testimony on the Hyde bill to stop babyselling, two prevailing attitudes were present among congressmen. First, some seemed determined to attach themselves to what the press termed "a sexy issue," for the publicity value alone. For example, one freshman congressman from California read a generalized statement on babyselling for the benefit of the reporters in attendance and then left. His concern about babyselling did not extend so far that he wished to waste any time listening to what others who testified had to say.

The second disturbing element was that some committee members appeared more concerned about those attorneys handling adoptions being able to collect their fees than they were about stopping the sale of children in this country.

Joseph Morello, who testified at those hearings, also noticed this latter attitude. As he put it, "The real problem is not to draft a law that will allow a lawyer to get his fee. No honest lawyer is going to be involved in what the baby lawyers are doing and nobody ought to draft a statute to protect a shady enterprise like that. If it means doing adoptions for free, so be it. It's really no work at all to do these adoptions. Law clerks could do it. I mean, you don't have to be Clarence Darrow or Oliver Wendell Holmes. In New York it's literally filling in the blanks and I can't imagine charging people more than a couple hundred bucks for this work."

The point is, however, that, as Senator Dodd said of his bill, there need be no prohibition against a lawyer's taking an *honest* fee for his work in an adoption. If he wants to profit as a babyfinder, then, yes, he will justifiably be in trouble.

It's terribly important for members of Congress to be aware of their constituents' feelings about babyselling. If they learn the public is not apathetic about it, that the voters want it stopped, then they will do something about it.

Federal legislation is definitely needed in order to control babyselling, but also needed is improvement in many state laws. In 1974, an interim study commission of the Iowa General Assembly held extensive hearings on adoption. An outgrowth of that committee's work was Iowa's Adoption Act of 1975, an act that had three important provisions which should be a part of all states' adoption laws.

According to Brice Oakley, a Clinton, Iowa attorney who chaired that committee, these provisions were:

1) A placement cannot be made until the prospective adoptive parents have been pre-investigated by the Department of Social Services or by an investigator selected by that department.

What this provision does is attempt to prevent children being placed into unsuitable homes from which it is virtually impossible to remove them. The hope is that, by pre-screening, poor or merely marginally suitable homes and parents will be eliminated and the child made all the safer.

2) Fees in conjunction with *any* placement must be usual, necessary, and commensurate with services rendered. The prospective parents are required to file a full financial disclosure with the adoption petition and criminal penalties are imposed for violations. Likewise, it is illegal for a natural parent to receive a fee for having a baby.

This effectively rules out buying a child and imposes penalties for perjury, which we have seen to be commonplace in black-market adoptions. It also bars the practice of baby making.

3) There must be close court supervision, through a mechanism of legal custody, at all stages of the adoption procedure.

This prevents the child from being shuffled around beyond the court's jurisdiction. In essence, this provision makes the other two workable, for without close court supervision and enforcement of sanctions, laws mean nothing. This is the problem Elizabeth Cole has cited over and over again. The courts seem either unaware of the problems involved in babyselling or else they just don't care about the situation. Iowa has attempted, in this third provision, to make the courts aware and concerned in *all* adoptions, not just those that may be based upon black-market transactions.

Though black-market adoption is not exactly rampant in Iowa, it has taken place. One family mentioned in Ronald Silverton's files was from Iowa, and Brice Oakley told about a client of his who was approached by the black market:

"One client made a contact with a friend from Washington, D.C. in conjunction with other business, and mentioned the desire to adopt. The word was out and, within a week, a lawyer from Texas called to inform this well-to-do and prominent couple of a healthy white child who was available. The couple had to decide if they wanted the child by the next day. The fee? Ten thousand dollars for legal services and other necessary expenses. Payment was to be one thousand dollars by check and nine thousand in cash."

Others among Oakley's clients have been contacted by black-market babysellers in California, New York, and Florida. So when Iowa studied alternative adoption laws, they took the black market into consideration and tried to prevent its further intrusion into the state. Before Oakley entered general practice he was an Iowa Assistant Attorney General assigned, in part, to the Department of Social Welfare. As an attorney he has placed more than one hundred and twenty-five children for adoption and has never found it necessary to charge more than four hundred dollars for his services. He has seen the adoption process from all sides—as a prosecutor, a legislator, and as an attorney handling adoptions—and the bill his committee brought to the floor of the Iowa House, and subsequently passed, is a testament to his expertise.

One legal problem not dealt with in the Iowa act, but which should be handled with some uniformity among the states, is that of terminating the rights of an illegitimate baby's natural father. In the landmark Supreme Court decision of 1971, Stanley *v*. Illinois, the high court ruled that unwed fathers do, indeed, have some rights to their children. In subsequent years, however, the extent of those rights has been interpreted in markedly different ways.

In virtually all black-market adoptions, the rights of the alleged father are simply ignored, creating a remote possibility that the adoption may someday be overturned by a natural father. The natural mothers are instructed to say they don't know who the father of their baby is, usually a false admission of promiscuity.

Some adoption agencies have reacted in the opposite extreme, assuming that any means, no matter how far-fetched, must be taken to locate the natural father and get his signature alongside the natural mother's before a child can be adopted. Many children have, therefore, been placed into foster care because their fathers cannot be readily located.

Unfortunately, some of the requirements of Stanley *v*.

Illinois have added to the baby shortage. In many cases, an unwed mother does not want to tell the father of her child that she is pregnant, much less have to ask for his signature on relinquishment papers. If she is forced to name him so that he can be contacted, she may well decide to keep her child instead.

Robert Burns had several seemingly valid complaints against the rules set down by Stanley v. Illinois. When asked if he always contacted the natural father and had him sign relinquishment papers he replied, "In most cases, if his address is known, I prepare a consent for him to sign. If he's out of state, I serve him by publication—it's published in the newspaper and he gets a copy from the court. If he is unknown or his address is unknown, we have to publish too.

"This really shouldn't be," Burns protested, "because a lot of times the boy who impregnates the girl doesn't really know. She leaves her town to avoid disgrace. No one in town knows. She's just a lovely girl who got caught. Yet we have to notify the putative father, which then ruins this girl's reputation and her future life. I think it's horrible."

California attorney David Leavitt also commented on the problems created by various interpretations of Stanley v. Illinois. "I've had a number of girls come to me where the father really has no right to stop the adoption," he said, "but some adoption agency has told them that if he doesn't sign, they can't have the baby adopted and it will go into foster care indefinitely. The mothers come to me in tears and say, 'How can they do that?'

"Well, the father can't stop the adoption. He may be entitled to know an adoption is going on, but he can't stop it."

How then does Leavitt go about having the natural father's rights terminated in his adoptions? "He may be asked to sign," Leavitt said. "If he doesn't, then we take it to court and the court enters an order that says he has no rights."

If the natural mother refuses to name the father, then, Leavitt said, there may be a danger to the validity of the adoption. "For a while, our judges here in Los Angeles would order the mother into court and inform her that if she refused to identify the father, they would put her in jail for contempt of court. This practice stopped in 1975. They never actually put a girl in jail."

If a girl refuses to name the father so that he can be asked to sign papers, Leavitt maintains it is still all right to go through with the adoption, informing the adoptive parents of the risks they may be taking.

In some independent adoptions, attorneys have moved the baby to another state in which the courts have adopted a looser interpretation of Stanley v. Illinois.

Elizabeth Cole spoke of some of the methods agencies have used to comply with the law: "The jurisdictions have gone wild trying to determine what this [notice to the putative father] is. And the methods of coping with this have been, for example, looking into the phone book for every man with a name similar to the alleged father's name and writing personal letters to everyone of that name, saying, 'Are you the father of Mary Jones's baby?' "

She illustrated just how ridiculous some of this has become: "In one jurisdiction they got a response from an eighty-four-year-old man who said, 'I am not the father of Mary Jones's baby, but wish that I were.' "

Ms. Cole said that the requirement of notifying the unwed father has also created problems of confidentiality for the natural mother. Ms. Cole sees it as a major impediment to the early placement of children.

"I think the father does have constitutional rights that should be safeguarded. But some of the extremes in the practice of safeguarding those rights have to be ruled out."

Helen Ramirez, director of the Los Angeles County Department of Adoption, which handles more adoptions than any other agency in the world, agreed that attempts to comply with Stanley v. Illinois have delayed the placement of children. She called for legislation that would clarify the rights of the natural father.

"We would like to see some procedure whereby natural fathers have to assume responsibility for coming forth and declaring paternity, saying they will take some responsibility prior to the birth of the child. If they do not," Ms. Ramirez said, "then we feel that their rights have been served, and we can go ahead and place the child if all the other legal requirements have been met."

There is obviously no easy solution to this problem. It would seem that, with a newborn infant, the father should have no rights unless he could prove he was either married to the mother or had lived with her as a common-law husband and wishes to take full responsibility for the child she cannot raise. A man should not be able to prevent his child from being adopted if he is unwilling to take on the responsibility of raising it himself. And, rationally speaking, of course, there is no way a man can prove fatherhood.

We do need, at the very least, some consistency among the states in the enforcement of notification and relinquishment procedures for unwed fathers, procedures designed to spare the natural mother as much embarrassment as possible while taking reasonable measures to identify and notify the natural father.

Probably a definition of the procedures required in notifying the putative father and gaining his consent to an adoption should be outlined in both state and federal law, so as to apply to both intrastate and interstate adoptions equally. It certainly would be helpful to know that one set of standards can be applied to *all* adoptions.

With strong federal legislation as well as improved state laws, coupled with court concern and awareness, black-market adoption can be essentially eradicated. The babysellers will either have to get out of the business or risk spending time in federal prison. And children who are adopted can be sure they are getting the best families available—not being sold to the highest bidder.

Enforcement of strong legislation can guarantee every adopted child at least a fighting chance for a happy life. Unfortunately, it won't guarantee a child to every couple who wants to adopt. A solution to the baby shortage is far less easy to find than a solution to babyselling.

There are some alternatives, though, for couples who truly want to experience parenthood. There may not be a bouncing blond, blue-eyed baby boy in every infertile couple's future, but there are children who can and should be adopted—children who want a family as much as these families want a child. The problem is to help them find each other.

CHAPTER EIGHT

Alternatives
to the Black Market

The baby black market has been caused mainly by the combination of a large demand for adoptable babies and a small supply, with a large number of unscrupulous profiteers thrown in. The demand for adoptable children will certainly not diminish markedly in the near future, nor will the supply of healthy white infants increase noticeably. And we need some powerful legal action to get rid of the profiteers.

There are alternatives to the black market, though, for people who want to experience parenthood and cannot have their own biological children.

Legitimate independent adoption may be one alternative for some couples in states where it is legal. But the supply of babies in the gray market is dwindling, too, although sometimes determination and aggression can pay off.

California adoption attorney David Leavitt has some tips for couples who come to him looking for adoptable children. He advises his clients to look for a baby themselves. Most couples do find their own child.

"The best source is obstetricians," he says. "The

largest number of independent adoptions originates in a doctor's office. Every year or two, an obstetrician will have a young patient who's pregnant and he'll generally call a couple he knows. So I tell my clients that if they're wise, they'll become known to as many OB's as possible."

A second source, Leavitt says, is other women. "When someone tells me they want to adopt," he said, "the first thing I tell them is, 'Make sure every woman you know is aware that you're looking for a baby,' because women learn about these things constantly. They have daughters in high school whose girl friends have had to go to schools for unwed mothers, or the next-door neighbor has a babysitter who's pregnant out of wedlock, or cousin Sue back in Topeka, Kansas, has a daughter who's got to get out of town because she's pregnant. They can't wait to call and tell you if they know you're looking."

Leavitt's advice apparently works for many of his clients, because he says about half of them find a baby to adopt within a year. "But remember," he said, "eighty percent of the placements [of healthy white infants] are private here. And my people represent only a small portion of the adopting public. The bulk of the public thinks private procedures are illegal or illegitimate or dangerous and they won't investigate, or, if they wanted to investigate, they wouldn't know whom to call. The overwhelming majority of people who want to adopt are standing in line at agencies."

Couples interested in independent adoption must be sure that the attorney or physician they approach is indeed ethical and legitimate, and not one who will try to edge them into the black market. The cases cited in this book give them a good basis on which to identify and eliminate the babysellers. If the fees are initially suspiciously high, or later begin to escalate, or if the "source" insists on supplying a baby born out of state when there seems no logical reason to do so, the earmarks of the black market are there. A smart couple will not only stay away from this kind of deal, but will report it to their local authorities as well.

Of course, legal independent adoption cannot be the solution for all—or even significantly many—couples who want to adopt. It will help only a few. The others must look elsewhere or forget about having children.

One basic problem is that many couples think of adoption only in terms of infants, only in terms of healthy infants, and only in terms of an infant who will grow up to look as if it were born to them. Given the realities of adoption today, any couple who really wants to be parents should be strongly urged to reassess their priorities. There *are* children available for adoption and there are thousands more who, hopefully, will soon be freed for adoption, both legally and financially. But most of them aren't healthy white infants. Rather, they are older children; children of minority racial and ethnic backgrounds; children with physical, mental, and emotional handicaps; and children who are members of sibling groups. It takes a special kind of thought process for a couple to shift its position from wishing to adopt a healthy white infant to, say, taking in a five-year-old biracial child with emotional problems. But, for the couple who truly wants to experience parenthood rather than merely wanting to conform to the life-style of their more fertile friends and their, perhaps, conservative social upbringing and mores, this alternative can be a most rewarding solution to both their problem and the child's.

It is estimated that there are at least four hundred and twenty-five thousand children currently in foster care in this country of whom at least one hundred and twenty thousand could be adopted. There remain various difficulties in freeing them, not the least of which is that nobody knows much about a great number of them. Many social workers simply do not recognize these children as adoptable, so they don't try to find families for them. As a result, the youngsters are often switched from foster home to foster home, living a tragic life and never really belonging anywhere.

Many social agencies are so overworked and under-staffed that they just do not keep track of the foster children for whom they are supposed to be responsible.

"I visited agencies," Elizabeth Cole said, "where case records of children were kept in cardboard boxes in the hall-ways, and there were records on 'children' twenty-five and twenty-six years old who were married and raising families of their own, but whom the system still listed as kids. The situation is tragic in that we cannot estimate how many children need permanent homes for adoption because of the lack of administrative and recording systems within the agency which will keep track of these children."

Some of the children in foster care are the victims of their emotionally bankrupt biological parents, parents whose sole contribution to their children's lives is to send them cards on their birthdays and Christmas. Unfortunately, the courts are usually reluctant to sever parental rights so that the children can be adopted and experience a real home life.

Ms. Cole cited several studies which found that un-less children are returned home within the first year, or year and a half, of their placement in foster care, their chances of ever being returned home are reduced to practically nil.

Yet terminating the biological parents' rights, even after that length of time, is difficult. "The agency seeks to terminate parental rights by going into court, saying this par-ent really has not fulfilled his or her obligation as a parent.

The court orders proof, which the agency cannot meet. Number one, it asks if you have worked with the parent to overcome the problems. And most agencies have to say no because they have not even seen the parent for two years."

Ms. Cole said that natural parents in this situation are often unwilling to sign the relinquishment papers that would give their children a chance for a permanent family for a "number of psychological reasons which are probably not clear to any one of us. They feel guilty about giving up the children and do not want to do so with complete finality. Perhaps this is the only degree of parenting they can cope with—parenting from a distance."

There are strong signs of change that may result in the freeing of thousands of children who have been stuck in foster care for years.

One example of this change is a broadening of the methods used to find families. Even when foster children are freed for adoption, there has been a geographical problem in finding them adoptive homes. Often, for instance, a sibling group of three might be in foster care in Georgia where there are no adoptive parents willing to take them in. Perhaps a couple in Oregon would love to have just such a ready-made family. But how do they find each other?

Solving this type of problem has been one job of the North American Center on Adoption. Among its programs is the Adoption Resource Exchange of North America (ARENA), which, since 1967, has been assisting adoption agencies in placing children for whom no permanent homes can be found in their own locality. This is done by maintaining a national registry of available families and children who seem suited to each other.

The North American Center on Adoption is also dedicated to removing legal, racial, and other obstacles that may stand between these waiting children and prospective parents.

Another hopeful sign of movement is that an excellent bill is currently before Congress that would help free for adoption thousands of children now in foster care by eliminating some of the barriers they face. It is co-sponsored by Senator Alan Cranston and Representative Yvonne B. Burke, both of California. Known as the Opportunities for Adoption Act, it was first introduced in 1974. Mrs. Burke described its purpose:

"My bill would add a new title XIV—'adoption assistance programs'—to the Public Health Services Act. It would address itself to three areas.

"First, it would promote the establishment of uniform adoption regulations in the United States in order to eliminate jurisdictional and legal obstacles to adoption (a point which would also help eliminate the black market). The bill would open the field for prospective adoptive parents to the nation as a whole rather than to individual states.

"Second, the legislation would provide federal financial assistance to states for the purpose of assisting adoption agencies and prospective adoptive parents in meeting certain costs of adoption in order to remove or alleviate the financial obstacles to adoption by qualified individuals.

"Finally, the bill provides for the establishment of a National Office of Adoption Information and Services within the Department of Health, Education, and Welfare to insure quality standards for adoption services and to provide for a national adoption information exchange system to match children in need of adoption with prospective adoptive parents."

One particularly essential aspect of the Cranston-

Burke bill is the provision for financial aid to both agencies and adoptive parents when needed to enable an adoption to take place. For example, often a couple is willing to adopt a physically-handicapped child, but cannot meet the medical expenses that child will incur. If the child remains in foster care, the government will pay medical expenses, but as soon as it is adopted, the adoptive parents are expected to absorb those costs. But the parents' personal health insurance will not cover preexisting conditions in the adopted child so if they do adopt such a child, they would be much worse off financially than if they had given birth to a handicapped child of their own. And, of course, the child, too, is worse off under these circumstances, since he will probably remain unadopted.

Since adoption is better for everyone involved—the couple who wants a child, the child, and our society—it would seem logical that public funds continue to pay medical expenses to insure the adoption. The total cost to the government would still be much, much less than if the child remained in foster care.

Hopefully, too, the financial help available to agencies under the Cranston-Burke bill would enable them to establish a workable system both for keeping track of children in foster care and for helping to get more of them freed for adoption.

Adoption of a child with special needs who is now in foster care, then, is for many couples a realistic alternative to the unrealistic dream of adopting a healthy white infant.

For couples who cannot cope with an older child who would come to them with established personality patterns, there are infants available from foreign countries, particularly Korea, the Philippines, and Colombia at the present time.

But, of course, most are not of Caucasian heritage. Couples interested in adopting a baby or youngster from a foreign country should contact their local county or private adoption agency. Costs of these adoptions will run somewhat higher than adoption of an American child, primarily because of the cost of transportation, but most agencies handling international adoptions use a sliding fee scale tied to the adoptive family's income.

Couples less positive that they can permanently take on a child who is not a healthy white infant might explore the possibility of becoming foster parents. Such a situation would give them a taste of parenthood and, in many instances, a child in foster care can later be adopted by its foster parents.

Reuben Pannor of Los Angeles' Vista Del Mar Child Care Service recommends foster parenting as an alternative to adoption for many childless couples. "There's a tremendous need for foster parents," he said, "but it's really misunderstood. When we suggest that a couple become foster parents, they often reject the idea because they say the child will just go back to his own parents and they couldn't take that.

"But some people have been foster parents for years and they're obviously getting a lot out of it. It's very rewarding to see a child grow, develop, become independent and go back to his family, then repeat the process with a new child. Besides," Pannor went on, "that's what happens with our own biological children. If we raise them correctly, they grow away from us and leave us."

According to Elizabeth Cole's statistics, if a child is in foster care for more than eighteen months, chances are he will never go back to his biological family. Given more enlightened judges presiding over our family courts, and legal action to sever parental rights when appropriate, such children should soon become available for adoption.

There are, then, alternatives to the black market for couples who truly want to be parents. They simply need to explore avenues other than the crowded ones leading to the handful of healthy white infants. There are children in foster care, children with special needs and problems, sibling groups, children from other countries and of minority racial and ethnic backgrounds.

What we need is to have enacted legislation such as that sponsored by Senator Alan Cranston and Representative Yvonne B. Burke. That's the first step.

The second step is to rethink what kind of child is adoptable and what kind of grouping can be a "normal" family. Both social workers and prospective adoptive parents must reassess their criteria.

For every couple who longs for a child, there is a child somewhere longing for parents.

They just need help finding each other.

APPENDIX

Adoption Sources

There are many sources of adoptable children in the United States. Although there are few healthy white infants available for adoption today, thousands of other children are waiting for loving homes.

Legitimate independent adoption is legal in forty-six states and is usually arranged directly with the natural mother or through an ethical attorney or physician. Families interested in independent adoption might contact their personal physician or attorney as a starting point, keeping in mind the pitfalls of independent adoption noted elsewhere in this book.

Families wishing to adopt through an agency are advised to contact their state department of welfare for a list of licensed agencies. An alternative method of finding a reputable agency is to contact a local member agency of the Child Welfare League of America, Incorporated. Accredited members of the League subscribe to a code of ethics, are licensed by their various states, are racially nondiscriminatory, and are financially sound. This appendix includes a list of League agencies that handle adoptions. Although every effort has been made to make the list up-to-date, changes do occur fairly frequently and families may wish to write the League's headquarters (67 Irving Place, New York, New York 10003) for a current list.

Two national organizations may also be of help to prospective adoptive parents:

The North American Center on Adoption, 67 Irving Place, New York, New York 10003. The Center is a nonprofit organization providing consultation to the adoptive establishment, assistance to adoption advocates, education to the general public, and exchange services to aid in the adoption of special needs youngsters.

The North American Council on Adoptable Children, 250 East Blaine, Riverside, California 92507. The Council is composed of adoptive parents and citizens concerned with the right of every child to a permanant family. Persons may write for a list of member organizations in their areas.

ALABAMA

Children's Aid Society
3600 South Eighth Avenue
Birmingham,
Alabama 35222
(205) 251-7148

ALASKA

Alaska Department of Health
and Social Services
State of Alaska, Pouch-H 01
Juneau, Alaska 99811
(907) 465-3005

ARIZONA

Family Service Agency
1530 East Flower Street

Phoenix, Arizona 85014
(602) 264-9891

Jewish Family and
Children's Service
2033 North Seventh Street
Phoenix, Arizona 85006
(602) 257-1904

Arizona Children's
Home Association
2700 South Eighth Avenue
Tucson, Arizona 85713
(602) 622-7611

CALIFORNIA

Children's Bureau of
Los Angeles
2824 Hyans Street

Los Angeles, Calif. 90026
(213) 384-2515

Branch Offices:

Centinela Valley:
463 W. Century Blvd.
Inglewood, California 90304
(213) 674-4450
San Fernando Valley:
6851 Lennox Avenue
Van Nuys, California 91405
(213) 785-8861

Children's Home Society of
California
(statewide voluntary)
3100 West Adams Blvd.
Los Angeles,
California 90018
(213) 733-1141, 735-1351

District Offices:

703 Truxtun Avenue
Bakersfield,
California 93301
(805) 324-4091

1216 Sheridan Avenue
Chico, California 95926
(916) 342-2464

507 "F" Street
Eureka, California 95501
(707) 442-8912

703 North Fulton
Fresno, California 93728
(209) 486-0355

125 East 14th Street
Long Beach,
California 90813
(213) 591-1313

3100 West Adams Blvd.
Los Angeles,

California 90018
(213) 733-1141, 735-1351

1128 "F" Street
Marysville, California 95901
(916) 742-8821

1012 "I" Street, Room 16
Modesto, California 95354
(209) 521-5237

444 Pearl Street
Monterey, California 93940
(408) 373-4126

3200 Telegraph Avenue
Oakland, California 94609
(415) 655-7406

135 West Magnolia
Oxnard, California 93030
(805) 486-0090

73-960 El Paseo
Palm Desert,
California 92260
(714) 346-4303

1050 Yuba Street
Redding, California 96001
(916) 243-9041

3903 Brockton Avenue
Riverside, California 92501
(714) 686-7603

3731 "T" Street
Sacramento,
California 95816
(916) 452-4672

7695 Cardinal Court
San Diego, California 92123
(714) 278-7800

3000 California Street
San Francisco,
California 94115
(415) 922-2803

1010 Ruff Drive
San Jose, California 95110
(408) 293-8940

300 South Sycamore Street
Santa Ana, California 92701
(714) 542-1147

824 Bath Street
Santa Barbara,
California 93101
(805) 962-9191

210 West Main St., Suite 6
Mail: P.O. Box 483
Santa Maria,
California 93454
(805) 925-0330

2211 Fourth Street, Office 8
Santa Rosa,
California 95404
(705) 528-9199

6851 Lennox Avenue
Van Nuys, California 91405
(213) 785-8861

11646 West Pico Blvd.
West Los Angeles,
California 90064
(213) 879-0910

Los Angeles County
Department of Adoptions
(local public)
2550 West Olympic Blvd.
Los Angeles,
California 90006
(213) 381-2761

Service Offices:

3405 West Imperial Hwy.
Inglewood,
California 90303
(213) 673-3800

44758 North Elm Street
Lancaster, California 93534
(805) 948-4615

120 East Ocean Blvd.
Long Beach,
California 90802
(213) 775-2721

8155 Van Nuys Blvd.
Panorama City,
California 91402
(213) 787-1850

644 El Segundo Blvd.
Los Angeles,
California 90059
(213) 538-5300

1502 West Covina
Parkway West
West Covina,
California 91790
(213) 338-8461

Vista Del Mar
Child Care Services
3200 Motor Avenue
Los Angeles,
California 90034
(213) 836-1223

COLORADO

Denver Department of
Social Services
(local public)
320 West Eighth Avenue
Denver, Colorado 80204
(303) 292-4100

Jewish Family and Children's
Service of Colorado
300 South Dahlia Street,
Suite 101
Denver, Colorado 80222
(303) 321-3115

CONNECTICUT

Family Services-
   Woodfield (Inc.)
   800 Clinton Avenue
   Bridgeport,
   Connecticut 06604
   (203) 368-4291

Catholic Family Services
   Archdiocese of Hartford
   244 Main Street
   Hartford,
   Connecticut 06106
   (203) 522-8241

Child and Family Services
   (regional voluntary)
   1680 Albany Avenue
   Hartford,
   Connecticut 06105
   (203) 236-4511

District Office:

110 Main Street
Manchester,
Connecticut 06040
(203) 643-2761

Department of Children and
   Youth Services
   (statewide public)
   345 Main Street
   Hartford,
   Connecticut 06115
   (203) 566-3537

Regional Offices:

434 State Street
Bridgeport,
Connecticut 06603
(203) 384-1761

110 Bartholomew Avenue
Hartford,

Connecticut 06115
(203) 566-4416

Main Street Extension
Middletown,
Connecticut 06457
(203) 347-4411

194 Bassett Street
New Haven,
Connecticut 06511
(203) 787-6181

279 Main Street
Norwich,
Connecticut 06360
(203) 889-2351

1642 Bedford Street
Stamford,
Connecticut 06457
(203) 348-9245

352 Main Street
Torrington,
Connecticut 06790
(203) 482-5531

79 Linden Street
Waterbury,
Connecticut 06702
(203) 573-1211

Jewish Family Service of
   Greater Hartford
   333 Bloomfield Avenue
   West Hartford,
   Connecticut 06117
   (203) 522-8265

Family Services, Inc.
   92 Vine Street
   New Britain,
   Connecticut 06052
   (203) 223-9291

District Office:

285 Main Street
Bristol, Connecticut 06010
(203) 583-9225

Child and Family Agency of
Southeastern Connecticut,
Inc. (provisional)
189 Williams Street
New London,
Connecticut 06320
(203) 443-2896

Family and Children's
Services, Inc.
60 Palmers Hill Road
Stamford,
Connecticut 06902
(203) 324-3167

Branch Offices:

41 Corbin Drive
Darien, Connecticut 06820
(203) 655-0547

103 South Avenue
New Canaan,
Connecticut 06840
(203) 972-0556
if no answer, call
(203) 324-3167

DELAWARE

Children's Bureau of Delaware
(statewide voluntary)
2005 Baynard Blvd.
Wilmington,
Delaware 19802
(302) 658-5177

*Branch Office (for Kent and
Sussex Counties):*

12 North West Front Street
Milford, Delaware 19963
(302) 422-8013

DISTRICT OF COLUMBIA

Family and Child Services of
Washington, D.C.
929 "L" Street, Northwest
Washington, D.C. 20001
(202) 232-6510

FLORIDA

Family Counseling Center of
Pinellas County, Inc.
Central Administrative
Office
2960 Roosevelt Blvd.
Clearwater, Florida 33520
(813) 536-9427

District Office:

928 22nd Avenue South
St. Petersburg,
Florida 33705
(813) 822-2961

The Children's Home Society
of Florida
(statewide voluntary)
3027 San Diego Road
P. O. Box 10097
Jacksonville, Florida 32207
(904) 396-4084

Offices:

Holiday Office Center,
Suite 195
1325 North Atlantic Avenue
Cocoa Beach, Florida 32931
(305) 783-2819

201 Osceola Avenue
Daytona Beach,
Florida 32014
(904) 255-7407

180

105 Northeast Third Street
Fort Lauderdale,
Florida 33301
(305) 763-6573

2517 Second Street
Fort Myers, Florida 33901
(813) 334-2008

1105 West University Blvd.
Gainesville, Florida 32601
(904) 376-5186

842 South Missouri Avenue
Lakeland, Florida 33801
(813) 688-7968

800 Northwest 15th Street
Miami, Florida 33136
(305) 324-1262

843 East Silver Springs Blvd.
Ocala, Florida 32670
(904) 629-7597

130 Pasadena Place
Orlando, Florida 32803
(305) 422-4441

5375 North Ninth Avenue
Pensacola, Florida 32504
(904) 476-3133

9721 Executive Center
Drive, Suite 140
St. Petersburg,
Florida 33702
(813) 576-2383

370 Office Plaza
P. O. Box 3474
Tallahassee, Florida 32303
(904) 877-5176

Catholic Service Bureau, Inc.
Archdiocese of Miami
(regional voluntary)

4949 Northeast Second Ave.
Miami, Florida 33137
(305) 754-2444

Regional Offices:

1300 South Andrews Ave.
Fort Lauderdale,
Florida 33316
(305) 522-2513

3211 Flagler Avenue
Key West, Florida 33040
(305) 296-8032

3196 Davis Blvd.
Naples, Florida 33940
(813) 774-6483

106 South Clematis Street
West Palm Beach,
Florida 33401
(305) 655-6342

United Family and
Children's Services, Inc.
2190 Northwest Seventh St.
Miami, Florida 33125
(305) 643-5700

Additional Offices:

Inner City Office
345 Northeast Second Ave.
Miami, Florida 33132
(305) 643-5700

South Dade Office
18861 South Dixie Highway
Miami, Florida 33157
(305) 232-1610

Jewish Family and
Children's Service
1790 Southwest 27th Ave.
Miami, Florida 33145
(305) 445-0555

District Offices:

420 Lincoln Road
Miami Beach,
Florida 33139
(305) 531-2363

850 Washington Avenue
Miami Beach,
Florida 33139
(305) 532-2446

2040 Northeast 163rd St.
North Miami Beach,
Florida 33162
(305) 949-6186

Social and Economic Services
Department of Health and
Rehabilitative Services
(statewide public)
1311 Winewood Blvd.
Building 5, Room 125
Tallahassee, Florida 32301
(904) 487-2380

GEORGIA

Child Service and
Family Counseling Center
1105 West Peachtree Street,
Northeast
Atlanta, Georgia 30309
(404) 873-6916

Branch Offices:

Bankhead Courts
Building 3513,
Apartment 418
Bankhead Highway
Atlanta, Georgia 30331
(404) 696-2471

East Lake Meadows
Building 280,
Apartment 1240

East Lake Blvd.
Atlanta, Georgia 30317
(404) 378-6241

Dunbar Center Office
477 Windsor Ave.,
Southwest
Atlanta, Georgia 30312
(404) 524-4544

Kirkwood Office
1599½ B Memorial Drive
Atlanta, Georgia 30317
(404) 373-4596

Florence Crittenton Services
P. O. Box 80369
Chamblee, Georgia 30341
(404) 457-5578

525 Marshall Street
Decatur, Georgia 30030
(404) 378-2543

Fairburn City
18-A Broad Street
Fairburn, Georgia 30213
(404) 964-9863

Cobb County
2050 Austell Road
Marietta, Georgia 30060
(404) 436-1567

Parent and Child Development
Services, Inc.
428 Bull Street
Savannah, Georgia 31401
(912) 234-2674

HAWAII

Child and Family Service
Community Service Center,
Suite 20
200 North Vineyard Blvd.
Honolulu, Hawaii 96817
(808) 521-2377

ILLINOIS

The Bensenville Home Society
331 South York Road
Bensenville, Illinois 60106
(312) 766-5800

Chicago Child Care Society
5467 University Avenue
Chicago, Illinois 60615
(312) 643-0452

Child and Family Services
234 South Wabash Avenue
Chicago, Illinois 60604
(312) 427-8790

District Offices:

Lawndale Homemaker
Service
3142 West Roosevelt
Chicago, Illinois 60624
(312) 722-1843

North Suburban
Homemaker Service
828 Davis Street
Evanston, Illinois 60201
(312) 864-6360

Northwest Suburban
Homemaker Service
410 North Arlington
Heights Road
Arlington Heights,
Illinois 60004
(312) 398-3388

South Suburban
Homemaker Service
157 East 155th Street
Harvey, Illinois 60426
(312) 339-4000

West Suburban Homemaker
Service

1011 Lake Street
Oak Park, Illinois 60302
(312) 383-5940

Homemaker Service of Lake
and McHenry Counties
509 East Park Avenue
Libertyville, Illinois 60048
(312) 362-0760

Evangelical Child and
Family Agency
127 North Dearborn Street
Chicago, Illinois 60602
(312) 372-9560

District Offices:

5010 West Chicago Avenue
Chicago, Illinois 60651
(312) 287-7033

105 North Maple Street
Elmhurst, Illinois 60126
(312) 372-9560

Illinois Children's Home and
Aid Society
(statewide voluntary)
1122 North Dearborn St.
Chicago, Illinois 60610
(312) 944-3313

Regional Offices:

1002 College Avenue
Alton, Illinois 62002
(618) 462-2714

Suite 425
Champaign Plaza
113 North Neil
Champaign, Illinois
(217) 359-8815

Early Childhood Develop-
ment Center
826 Ridge Avenue

Evanston, Illinois 60202
(312) 866-8880

Evanston Children's Home
826 Ridge Avenue
Evanston, Illinois 60202
(312) 866-9554

304 North Main Street
Rockford, Illinois 61101
(815) 962-1043

South Side Office
10801 South Halsted Street
Chicago, Illinois 60628
(312) 468-0200

4 South Genesee Street
Room 414
Waukegan, Illinois 60085
(312) 662-5557

Jewish Children's Bureau
of Chicago
1 South Franklin Street
Chicago, Illinois 60606
(312) 346-6700

Lake Bluff/Chicago Homes for
Children (regional
voluntary)
200 Scranton Avenue
Lake Bluff, Illinois 60044
(312) 295-2360, 295-2220

Bethany Home
220 11th Avenue
Moline, Illinois 61265
(309) 797-7700

Counseling and Family Service
1821 North Knoxville Ave.
Peoria, Illinois 61603
(309) 685-5287

Branch Offices:

Northside Outreach
Counseling Office

800 Northeast Madison
Peoria, Illinois 61603
(309) 671-5215

Taft Homes
245 Green Street
Peoria, Illinois 61603
(309) 673-4340

YWCA
315 Buena Vista
Pekin, Illinois 61554
(309) 347-2104

Washington-Morton-Eureka
City Building
115 West Jefferson
Washington, Illinois 61571
(309) 283-3196

Lutheran Child and Family
Services (statewide
voluntary)
7620 Madison Street
River Forest, Illinois 60305
(312) 287-4848

Additional Locations:

Lutherbrook Children's
Center
343 West Lake Street
Addison, Illinois 60101
(312) 543-6900

2408 Lebanon Avenue
Belleville, Illinois 62221
(618) 234-8904

Chicago South
6253 South Michigan Ave.
Chicago, Illinois 60637
(312) 363-0667

Chicago-Loop
59 East Van Buren Street
Chicago, Illinois 60605
(312) 939-0930

1229 South Sixth Street
Springfield, Illinois 62703
(217) 544-4631

Illinois Department of
Children and Family
Services
623 East Adams Street
Springfield, Illinois 62706
(217) 782-7615

Regional Offices:

48 West Galena Blvd.
Aurora, Illinois 60504
(312) 896-0881

2125 South First Street
Champaign, Illinois 61820
(217) 333-1037

1439 South Michigan
Avenue
Chicago, Illinois 60605
(312) 341-7617

4320 West Montrose
Chicago, Illinois 60641
(312) 282-9470

950 East 61st Street
Chicago, Illinois 60637
(312) 793-4697

1026 South Damen
Chicago, Illinois 60612
(312) 793-4697

119 West Williams
Decatur, Illinois 62523
(217) 429-5731

Regional State Office Bldg.
10 Collinsville Avenue
East St. Louis, Illinois 62201
(618) 875-9300, ext. 235

58 North Chicago Street
Joliet, Illinois 60431
(815) 727-7675

2209 West Main Street
Marion, Illinois 62959
(618) 997-4371

2810 41st Street
Moline, Illinois 61265
(309) 762-9446

633 La Salle, Suite 301
Ottawa, Illinois 61350
(815) 433-4610

5415 North University
Peoria, Illinois 61614
(309) 691-2200, ext. 531

410 North Ninth Street
Quincy, Illinois 62301
(217) 223-7187

4302 North Main
Rockford, Illinois 61105
(815) 987-7640

205 East Locust Street
Salem, Illinois 62881
(618) 548-1692

4500 South Sixth Street Rd.
Springfield, Illinois 62706
(217) 786-6830

6th Floor, Waukegan Bldg.
4 South Genesee
Waukegan, Illinois 60085
(312) 244-4640

INDIANA

Family and Children's Service
305 South Third Avenue
Evansville, Indiana 47708
(812) 425-5181

Family and Children's Services
2424 Fairfield Avenue
Fort Wayne, Indiana 46807
(219) 744-4326

Jewish Family and Children's
Services, Inc.
1475 West 86th Street
Indianapolis, Indiana 46260
(317) 255-6641

Children's Bureau of
Indianapolis
615 North Alabama Street
Indianapolis, Indiana 46204
(317) 634-6481

Family and Children's Center
(statewide voluntary)
1411 Lincoln Way West
Mishawaka, Indiana 46544
(219) 259-5666

IOWA

Family and Children's Service
of Davenport
115 West Sixth Street
Davenport, Iowa 52803
(319) 323-1853

Iowa Children's and Family
Services (statewide
voluntary)
1101 Walnut
Des Moines, Iowa 50309
(515) 288-1981

Branch Office:

1216 Central Avenue
Fort Dodge, Iowa 50501

Iowa Department of Social
Services (statewide public)
Lucas State Office Building
Des Moines, Iowa 50319
(515) 281-5452

Lutheran Social Service of
Iowa (statewide voluntary)
3116 University Ave.
Des Moines, Iowa 50311
(515) 277-4476

Branch Offices:

Northeast:
1510 Logan
Waterloo, Iowa 50703
(319) 233-3579

North Central:
1327 Sixth Street Southwest
Mason City, Iowa 50401
(515) 423-6313

Northwest:
1312 Morningside Avenue
Sioux City, Iowa 51106
(712) 276-1073

Southeast:
1500 Sycamore
Iowa City, Iowa 52240
(319) 351-4880

Florence Crittenton Home
1105 28th Street
Sioux City, Iowa 51104
(712) 255-4321, 255-9620

KANSAS

Kansas Children's Service
League (statewide
voluntary)
P.O. Box 517
Wichita, Kansas 67201
(316) 942-4261

Branch Offices:

Black Adoption Program
and Services
1125 North Fifth

Kansas City, Kansas 66101
(913) 621-2016

P.O. Box 5314
Topeka, Kansas 66605
(913) 232-0543

KENTUCKY

Department for Human
  Resources
  Room 237, Capitol Annex
  Frankfort, Kentucky 40601
  (502) 564-7130

Branch Office:

Bureau for Social Services
Bush Building
Frankfort, Kentucky 40601
(502) 564-4650

Department of Social Services
Division of Children's
  Services (local public)
115 Cisco Road
Lexington, Kentucky 40504
(606) 253-1581

LOUISIANA

Health and Human Resources
  Administration (statewide
  public)
P.O. Box 44065
Baton Rouge,
Louisiana 70804
(504) 389-6036

Regional Offices:

P.O. Box 832
Alexandria,
Louisiana 71301
(318) 487-4511

Baton Rouge Region
Sub-Office

P.O. Box 206
Amite, Louisiana 70422
(504) 748-2421

Watkins Building
2843 Victoria Drive
Baton Rouge,
Louisiana 70805
(504) 389-7161

302 Jefferson Street
Lafayette, Louisiana 70501
(318) 233-4211

Lafayette Region Sub-Office
P.O. Box 1807
Lake Charles,
Louisiana 70601
(318) 433-0421

4th Floor, State Office Bldg.
122 St. John Street
Monroe, Louisiana 71201
(318) 322-6121

P.O. Box 13276
Broadmoor Station
New Orleans,
Louisiana 70125
(504) 486-3761

1237 Murphy Street
Shreveport,
Louisiana 71101
(318) 424-6461

Baton Rouge Region Sub-
  Office
P.O. Box 797
Thibodaux,
Louisiana 70301
(504) 447-7277

Children's Bureau of
  New Orleans
  Carondelet Building,
  Suite 801

226 Carondelet Street
New Orleans,
Louisiana 70130
(504) 525-2366

MAINE

Maine Department of Human
Services (statewide public)
State House
Augusta, Maine 04333
(207) 289-3456

District Offices:

Capital Shopping Center
Western Avenue
Augusta, Maine 04330
(207) 289-2851

117 Broadway
Bangor, Maine 04401
(207) 947-0511

373 Main Street
Caribou, Maine 04736
(207) 498-8151

415 Water Street
Ellsworth, Maine 04605
(207) 667-5361

38 Pleasant Street
Fort Kent, Maine 04743
(207) 834-3934

5 Mechanic Street
Houlton, Maine 04730
(207) 532-9531

179 Lisbon Street
Lewiston, Maine 04240
(207) 783-9151

Main Street
Machias, Maine 04654
(207) 255-3366

509 Forest Avenue
Portland, Maine 04111
(207) 774-4581

1 Park Drive
Rockland, Maine 04841
(207) 594-2521

76 Madison Avenue
Skowhegan, Maine 04976
(207) 474-5551

Community Counseling Center
187 Middle Street
Portland, Maine 04111
(207) 774-5727

Division Offices:

349 Brown Street
Westbrook, Maine 04092
(207) 854-8510

Parish House
First Parish Church
39 School Street
Gorham, Maine 04038
(207) 839-4277

279 Ocean House Road
Cape Elizabeth, Maine
04107
(207) 799-7339

MARYLAND

Baltimore City Department of
Social Services (local
public)
1510 Guilford Avenue
Baltimore, Maryland 21202
(301) 234-2201

Family and Children's Society
204 West Lanvale Street
Baltimore, Maryland 21217
(301) 669-9000

Specialized Children's
Services
1301 Park Avenue
Baltimore, Maryland 21217
(301) 669-9000

Branch Offices:

934 West Street
Annapolis, Maryland 21401
(301) 263-5743

2502 St. Paul Street
Baltimore, Maryland 21218
(301) 366-1430

1310 South Charles Street
Baltimore, Maryland 21230
(301) 752-0445

Jewish Family and Children's
Service
5750 Park Heights Avenue
Baltimore, Maryland 21215
(301) 466-9200

Branch Office:

5310 Old Court Road
Randallstown,
Maryland 21133

Baltimore County Department
of Social Services
(local public)
620 York Road
Towson, Maryland 21204
(301) 494-2520

Maryland Children's Aid and
Family Service Society, Inc.
(statewide voluntary)
303 West Chesapeake Ave.
Towson, Maryland 21204
(301) 825-3700
(800) 492-4704 toll-free
from Maryland communities

District Offices:

Baltimore County—Central:
303 West Chesapeake Ave.
Towson, Maryland 21204
(301) 825-3705

Baltimore County—East:
6905 Dunmanway
Dundalk, Maryland 21222
(301) 285-7300

Baltimore County—West:
623 Edmondson Avenue
Catonsville,
Maryland 21228
(301) 788-4944

Carroll County:
22 North Court Street
Westminster,
Maryland 21157
(301) 876-1233

Cecil County
(Cecil Center):
Holly Hall
Box 447
Elkton, Maryland 21921
(301) 398-4060

Eastern Shore:
205 Earle Avenue
Easton, Maryland 21601
(301) 822-1630

Harford County:
6 South Main Street
Bel Air, Maryland 21014
(301) 838-9000

Howard County:
8654 Baltimore National
Pike
Ellicott City,
Maryland 21043
(301) 461-1277

Kent County:
400 High Street
Chestertown,
Maryland 21620
(301) (0) Operator EN
9-4060

Western Maryland:
Cumberland,
Maryland 21502
(301) 722-6421

MASSACHUSETTS

Boston Children's
Service Association
1, 3, and 5 Walnut Street
Boston,
Massachusetts 02108
(617) 227-3800

Branch Office:

Baird Center
Ship Pond Road
RFD 6 Box 213
Plymouth,
Massachusetts 02360
(617) 224-8041

Jewish Family and
Children's Service
31 New Chardon Street
Boston,
Massachusetts 02114
(617) 227-6641

Massachusetts Department of
Public Welfare
(statewide public)
600 Washington Street
Boston,
Massachusetts 02111
(617) 727-6190
Adoption Placement Unit
(617) 727-6133

Regional Offices:

43 Hawkins Street
Boston,
Massachusetts 02111
(617) 227-8320

39 Boylston Street
Boston,
Massachusetts 02116
(617) 357-8250

1 Mill Street
Lawrence,
Massachusetts 01840
(617) 686-3971

684 Purchase Street
New Bedford,
Massachusetts 02740
(617) 997-3361

235 Chestnut Street
Springfield,
Massachusetts 01103
(413) 781-7510

75 A Grove Street
Worcester,
Massachusetts 01605
(617) 791-8571

The New England Home for
Little Wanderers
(statewide voluntary)
161 Huntington Ave. South
Boston,
Massachusetts 02130
(617) 232-8600

Parents' and Children's
Services of the
Children's Mission
329 Longwood Avenue
Boston,
Massachusetts 02115
(617) 232-7950

Children's Aid and Family
Society of Haverhill
69 Summer Street
Haverhill,
Massachusetts 01830
(617) 372-8516

Florence Crittenton
League, Inc.
201 Thorndike Street
Lowell,
Massachusetts 01852
(617) 452-9671

Catholic Family Services of
Greater Lynn
55 Lynn Shore Drive
Lynn, Massachusetts 01902
(617) 593-2312

Family and Children's
Service of Greater Lynn
111 North Common Street
Lynn, Massachusetts 01902
(617) 598-5517

New Bedford Child and
Family Service
141 Page Street
New Bedford,
Massachusetts 02740
(617) 996-8572

Children's Aid and Family
Service of Hampshire
County
8 Trumbull Road
Northampton,
Massachusetts 01060
(413) 584-5690

The Berkshire Center for
Families and Children
472 West Street
Pittsfield,
Massachusetts 01201
(413) 448-8281

Worcester Children's
Friend Society
21 Cedar Street
Worcester,
Massachusetts 01609
(617) 753-5425

MICHIGAN

Lutheran Children's
Friend Society of Michigan
304 Tuscola Road
P. O. Box B
Bay City, Michigan 48706
(517) 892-1539

Branch Offices:

10811 Puritan Avenue
Detroit, Michigan 48238
(313) 341-1121

2000 32nd Street South
Grand Rapids,
Michigan 49508
(616) 452-4921

Child and Family Services
of Michigan, Inc.
(statewide voluntary)
9880 East Grand River Ave.
Brighton, Michigan 48116
(313) 227-1191

Branch Offices:

Family Counseling and
Children's Services of
Lenawee County
213 Toledo Street
Adrian, Michigan 49221
(313) 265-5352

Child and Family Services of
Michigan, Inc.
309 Lockwood
Alpena, Michigan 49707
(517) 356-4567

Child and Family Service of
Washtenaw County
2301 Platt Road
Ann Arbor, Michigan 48104
(313) 971-6520

Ann Arbor Field Offices:

880 Wing Street
Plymouth, Michigan 48170
(313) 453-0890

131 East Michigan
Saline, Michigan 48176
(313) 429-4570

118 South Washington St.
Ypsilanti, Michigan 48197
(313) 483-1418

Family and Children's Service
of Calhoun County
182 West Van Buren
Battle Creek,
Michigan 49014
(616) 965-3247

Child and Family Services of
Michigan, Inc.
202 East Boulevard Drive
Flint, Michigan 48503
(313) 234-3671

Child and Family Services of
Michigan, Inc.
680 Washington Avenue
Holland, Michigan 49423
(616) 396-2301

Child and Family Services of
Michigan
Berriman Building, Suite 8
121 South Barnard
Howell, Michigan 48843
(517) 546-7530

Family Service and Children's
Aid of Jackson County

729 West Michigan Avenue
Jackson, Michigan 49201
(517) 782-8191

Family and Children's Service
of the Kalamazoo Area
1608 Lake Street
Kalamazoo,
Michigan 49001
(616) 344-0202

Family and Children's Services
of the Capitol Area, Inc.
300 North Washington
Lansing, Michigan 48933
(517) 484-4455

Child and Family Services of
the Upper Peninsula
109 Harlow Block
Postal Drawer A
Marquette, Michigan 49855
(906) 226-2516

Marquette Field Office:

322 Sheldon Avenue
Houghton, Michigan 49931
(906) 428-4488

Family and Children's Service
of Midland
116 Harold Street
Midland, Michigan 48640
(517) 631-5390

Children's Aid and Family
Service of Macomb
County, Inc.
57 Church Street
Mt. Clemens,
Michigan 48043
(313) 468-2656

Child and Family Services of
Michigan, Inc.
Box 763

717 Griswold Street
Port Huron,
Michigan 48060
(313) 982-5631

Child and Family Services
of Michigan
2000 South State Street
St. Joseph, Michigan 49085
(616) 983-5545

Michigan Children's Aid and
Family Services
210 Beaumont Place
Traverse City,
Michigan 49684
(616) 946-8975

Traverse City Field Offices:

124½ East Mitchell
Cadillac, Michigan 49601
(616) 775-8861

603 East Lake
Petoskey, Michigan 49770
(616) 347-4463

Jewish Family Service
24123 Greenfield Road
Southfield, Michigan 48075
(313) 559-1500

Methodist Children's Home
Society
(statewide voluntary)
26645 West Six Mile Road
Detroit, Michigan 48240
(313) 531-4060

State Department of Social
Services (statewide public)
Commerce Center
300 South Capitol Avenue
Lansing, Michigan 48926
(517) 373-2000

Catholic Social Services of
Macomb County
235 South Gratiot Avenue
Mount Clemens,
Michigan 48043
(313) 468-2616

Children's Aid and Family
Service of Macomb
County, Inc.
57 Church Street
Mount Clemens,
Michigan 48043
(313) 468-2656

Child and Family Services and
Muskegon Children's Home
1352 Terrace Street
Muskegon, Michigan 49442
(616) 726-3582

Family and Children Services
of Oakland
50 Wayne Street
Pontiac, Michigan 48058
(313) 332-8352

Branch Offices:

2351 West Twelve Mile Rd.
Berkley, Michigan 48072
(313) 548-8411

1374 East West Maple Road
Walled Lake, Michigan
(313) 624-3811

Catholic Social Services of
St. Clair County
P. O. Box 287
Port Huron,
Michigan 48060
(313) 985-8162

Catholic Social Services of
Oakland County
1424 East Eleven Mile Road

Royal Oak, Michigan 48067
(313) 548-4044

Branch Offices:

53 Franklin Blvd.
Pontiac, Michigan 48053
(313) 332-8375

1836 North Milford Road
Highland, Michigan 48031

5913 Dixie Highway
Waterford, Michigan 48095

1160 Myrtle
Pontiac Township,
Michigan 48053

Child and Family Service of
Saginaw County
1110 Howard Street
Saginaw, Michigan 46801
(517) 753-8491

MINNESOTA

Children's Home Society of
Minnesota
(statewide voluntary)
2230 Como Avenue
St. Paul, Minnesota 55108
(612) 646-6393

Minnesota Department of
Public Welfare
(statewide public)
Centennial Building
St. Paul, Minnesota 55155
(612) 296-2701
Direct services are pro-
vided by local departments.
For information, write Di-
rector, Division of Social
Services.

MISSISSIPPI

Mississippi State Department
of Welfare
(statewide public)
Box 4321
Fondren Station
Jackson, Mississippi 39216
(601) 982-6265
Direct services are pro-
vided by local departments.
For information, write Di-
rector, Division of Social
Services.

MISSOURI

Missouri Department of Social
Services (statewide public)
State Office Building
Jefferson City,
Missouri 65101
(314) 751-3221

Family and Children Services
of Kansas City, Inc.
3515 Broadway
Kansas City, Missouri 64111
(816) 753-5280

Branch Offices:

Eastern Jackson County:
1205 South Osage
Independence,
Missouri 64055
(816) 254-4343

Clay and Platte Counties:
6317 Northeast Antioch
Road, Suite 304
Kansas City,
Missouri 64119
(816) 454-4819

Northeast Johnson County:
5750 West 95th Street,
Suite 140
Overland Park,
Kansas 66207
(913) 642-4300

Linwood Multi-Purpose
Center
3200 Wayne
Kansas City,
Missouri 64109
(816) 924-6900

Jewish Family and Children
Services
1115 East 65th Street
Kansas City,
Missouri 64131
(816) 333-1172

Catholic Charities of St. Louis
4140 Lindell Blvd.
St. Louis, Missouri 63108
(314) 371-4980

Division of Children's
Services (local public)
929 North Spring Avenue
St. Louis, Missouri 63108
(314) 535-2670

Family and Children's Service
of Greater St. Louis
2650 Olive Street
St. Louis, Missouri 63103
(314) 371-6500

District Offices:

107 South Meramec
Clayton, Missouri 63105
(314) 727-3235

9811 West Florissant
St. Louis, Missouri 63136
(314) 521-6464

1360 South Fifth
St. Charles, Missouri 63301
(314) 946-6636

9109 Watson Road
St. Louis, Missouri 63126
(314) 968-2870

Jewish Family and
Children's Service
9385 Olive Blvd.
St. Louis, Missouri 63132
(314) 993-1000

Edgewood Children's Center
330 North Gore Avenue
Webster Groves,
Missouri 63119
(314) 968-2060

MONTANA

Department of Social and
Rehabilitative Services
(statewide public)
P. O. Box 1723
Helena, Montana 59601
(406) 449-3451

District Offices:

1211 Grand Avenue
Billings, Montana 59102
(406) 245-6453

P. O. Box 396
Butte, Montana 59701
(406) 792-2323

P. O. Box 472
Glasgow, Montana 59230
(406) 228-2331

1818 10th Avenue, South
Suite 1
Great Falls, Montana 59401
(406) 452-7837

25 South Ewing, Room 208
Helena, Montana 59601
(406) 449-2578

P. O. Box 216
Kalispell, Montana 59901
(406) 756-2942

P. O. Box 880
Miles City, Montana 59301
(406) 232-1385

Room 102, 818 Burlington
Missoula, Montana 59801
(406) 549-2754

NEBRASKA

Department of Public Welfare
(statewide public)
1526 K Street, 4th Floor
Lincoln, Nebraska 68508
(402) 471-2366

NEW HAMPSHIRE

Child and Family Services of
New Hampshire
P. O. Box 448
Manchester,
New Hampshire 03105
(603) 668-1920

Regional Offices:

1 Thompson Street
Concord,
New Hampshire 03301
(603) 224-7479

99 Hanover Street
Manchester,
New Hampshire 03105
(603) 688-1920

NEW JERSEY

The Children's Home Society
of New Jersey

(statewide voluntary)
929 Parkside Avenue
Trenton, New Jersey 08618
(609) 695-6274

NEW MEXICO

New Mexico Department of
Health and Social Services
(statewide public)
P. O. Box 2348
Santa Fe,
New Mexico 87503
(505) 827-2371

NEW YORK

Albany Home for Children
60 Academy Road
Albany, New York 12208
(518) 449-8870

Family and Children's Service
of Albany
12 South Lake Avenue
Albany, New York 12203
(518) 462-6531

State Department of Social
Services (statewide public)
1450 Western Avenue
Albany, New York 12203
(518) 457-7354
Direct Services are provided
by local departments. For
information, write Deputy
Commissioner, Division of
Services.

Child and Family Services
330 Delaware Avenue
Buffalo, New York 14202
(716) 849-1515

Jewish Family Service of
Erie County

775 Main Street
Buffalo, New York 14203
(716) 853-9956

The Children's Village
(nationwide voluntary)
Dobbs Ferry,
New York 10522
(914) 693-0600

Family Services of
Chemung County
709 John Street
Elmira, New York 14901
(607) 733-5696

Graham Home for Children
1 South Broadway
Hastings-on-Hudson,
New York 10706
(914) 478-1100

The Family and Children's
Home Society of Broome
County
257 Main Street
Binghamton,
New York 13905
(607) 729-6207

The Children's Home of
Kingston
26 Grove Street
Kingston, New York 12401
(914) 331-1448

Brookwood Child Care
363 Adelphi Street
Brooklyn, New York 11238
(212) 783-2610

The Children's Aid Society
105 East 22nd Street
New York,
New York 10010
(212) 949-4800

Jewish Child Care Association
of New York
345 Madison Avenue
New York,
New York 10017
(212) 490-9160

Louise Wise Services
12 East 94th Street
New York,
New York 10028
(212) 876-3050

The Salvation Army-Social
Services for Children
50 West 23rd Street
New York,
New York 10010
(212) 255-9400

The Spence-Chapin Services
to Families-Children
6 East 94th Street
New York,
New York 10028
(212) 369-0300

Branch Office:

Harlem-Dowling
Children's Services
2090 Seventh Avenue
New York,
New York 10027
(212) 749-3656
Serves Harlem and neigh-
boring communities.

Talbot Perkins
Children's Services
342 Madison Avenue
Suite 1717
New York,
New York 10017
(212) 697-1420

The Family and Children's
Service of Niagara Falls,
New York, Inc.
826 Chilton Avenue
Niagara Falls,
New York 14301
(716) 285-6984

Branch Office:

88 East Avenue
Lockport, New York 14094
(716) 433-6019

Hillside Children's Center
(statewide voluntary)
1183 Monroe Avenue
Rochester, New York 14620
(716) 473-5150

Monroe County Department
of Social Services
(local public)
111 Westfall Road
Rochester, New York 14620
(716) 442-4000

Adoption and Children's
Services of Westchester
19 Greenridge Avenue
White Plains,
New York 10605
(914) 949-6021

Westchester County
Department of Social
Services (local public)
Division of Services
County Office Bldg. No. 2
150 Grand Street
White Plains,
New York 10601
(914) 682-2871

NORTH CAROLINA

The Children's Home Society
of North Carolina

(statewide voluntary)
P. O. Box 6587
740 Chestnut Street
Greensboro,
North Carolina 27405
(919) 274-1538

District Offices:

84–86 Victoria Road
Room A-3
Asheville,
North Carolina 28801
(704) 258-1661

P. O. Box 2634
1801 East Franklin
Chapel Hill,
North Carolina 27514
(919) 929-4708

301 South Brevard
Charlotte,
North Carolina 28202
(704) 372-7170

Suite 205
Medical Arts Building
907 Hay Street
Fayetteville,
North Carolina 28305
(919) 483-8913

P. O. Box 494
Wilcar Building
219 West 10th Street
Greenville,
North Carolina 27834
(919) 752-5847

713 Princess Street
Wilmington,
North Carolina 28401
(919) 763-9727

State of North Carolina
Department of Human
Resources

Division of Social Services
(statewide public)
325 North Salisbury Street
Raleigh,
North Carolina 27611
(919) 733-3055
Direct services are provided
by local county departments
of social services. For information, write Head, Chil-
dren's Services Branch.

OHIO

Catholic Service League
of Akron
640 North Main Street
Akron, Ohio 44310
(216) 762-7481

Family and Children's Service
Society of Summit County
90 North Prospect Street
Akron, Ohio 44304
(216) 762-7601

Summit County Children's
Services Board
(local public)
264 South Arlington Street
Akron, Ohio 44306
(216) 379-5900

Family Counseling Services
618 Second St., Northwest
Canton, Ohio 44703
(216) 454-7066

Geauga County Department
of Welfare (local public)
13281 Ravenna Road
Chardon, Ohio 44024
(216) 285-9141

Jewish Family Service
1710 Section Road

Cincinnati, Ohio 45237
(513) 351-3680

The Children's Home of
Cincinnati, Ohio
5051 Duck Creek Road
Cincinnati, Ohio 45227
(513) 272-2800

Children's Services
1001 Huron Road
Cleveland, Ohio 44115
(216) 781-2043

Jewish Children's Bureau
21811 Fairmount Blvd.
Cleveland, Ohio 44118
(216) 932-2800

Lutheran Children's Aid
Society (regional voluntary)
4100 Franklin Avenue
Cleveland, Ohio 44113
(216) 281-2500

Family Counseling and
Crittenton Services
199 South Fifth Street
Columbus, Ohio 43215
(614) 221-7608

Additional Offices:

Crittenton Service Center:
4666 Sunbury Road
Columbus, Ohio 43219
(614) 471-7718

Family Counseling Center
East:
3901 East Livingston Ave.
Columbus, Ohio 43227
(614) 236-8733

Family Counseling Center
North:
733 East Granville Road

199

Columbus, Ohio 43229
(614) 885-8259

Family Counseling Center
Northwest:
3250 Riverside Drive
Columbus, Ohio 43221
(614) 486-6588

Family Life Center:
1393 East Broad Street
Columbus, Ohio 43205
(614) 253-7394

Getting Ready Center:
2220 Albert Avenue
Columbus, Ohio 43224
(614) 471-7718

Jewish Family Service
1175 College Avenue
Columbus, Ohio 43209
(614) 237-7686

Family Service Association
184 Salem Avenue
Dayton, Ohio 45406
(513) 222-9481

District Offices:

328 North Maple Street
Eaton, Ohio 45320
(513) 456-4697

16 South Pleasant Street
Fairborn, Ohio 45385
(513) 879-2061

22 East Central, Room 2
Miamisburg, Ohio 45342
(513) 222-9481

50 South Detroit Street,
Room 303
Xenia, Ohio 45385
(513) 426-4584 or
372-4611

The Child and Family
Service, Inc.
616 South Collett Street
Lima, Ohio 45805
(419) 225-1040

Beech Brook
3737 Lander Road
Pepper Pike, Ohio 44124
(216) 831-2255

Lutheran Social Services of
Northwestern Ohio
2149 Collingwood Blvd.
Toledo, Ohio 43620
(419) 243-9178

Trumbull County Children
Services Board
(local public)
Reeves Road Northeast
Warren, Ohio 44483
(216) 372-2010

Children's and Family Service
420 Oak Hill
Youngstown, Ohio 44502
(216) 743-3196

OKLAHOMA

State Department of
Institutions, Social and
Rehabilitative Services
(statewide public)
P. O. Box 25352
Oklahoma City, Oklahoma
73125
Division of Social Services
(405) 521-3531

Sunbeam Home and Family
Service
616 Northwest 21st Street
Oklahoma City,
Oklahoma 73103
(405) 528-7721

OREGON

The Boys and Girls Aid Society
of Oregon
(statewide voluntary)
2301 Northwest Glisan St.
Portland, Oregon 97210
(503) 222-9661

Department of Human
Resources
Children's Services Division
516 Public Service Building
Salem, Oregon 97310
(503) 378-4374

PENNSYLVANIA

Department of Public Welfare
(statewide public)
Health and Welfare Building
Harrisburg,
Pennsylvania 17120
Direct services are provided
by local departments. For
information, write Com-
missioner, Office of Children and Youth.

Family and Children's Service
of Harrisburg
121 Locust Street
Harrisburg,
Pennsylvania 17101
(717) 238-8118

Family and Children's Service
of Lancaster County
630 Janet Avenue
Lancaster,
Pennsylvania 17601
(717) 397-5241

Child Care Service of
Delaware County
(local public)

Front and Orange Streets
Media, Pennsylvania 19063
(215) 891-2501

Association for Jewish
Children
1301 Spencer Street
Philadelphia,
Pennsylvania 19141
(215) 549-9000

Children's Aid Society of
Pennsylvania
(regional voluntary)
311 South Juniper Street
Philadelphia,
Pennsylvania 19107
(215) 546-2990

Catholic Social Services of
Allegheny County
239 Fourth Avenue
Pittsburgh,
Pennsylvania 15222
(412) 281-4343

Jewish Family and
Children's Service
234 McKee Place
Pittsburgh,
Pennsylvania 15213
(412) 683-4900

RHODE ISLAND

Rhode Island Department of
Social and Rehabilitative
Services (statewide public)
600 New London Avenue
Cranston,
Rhode Island 02920
(401) 464-2121

St. Mary's Home for Children
420 Fruit Hill Avenue
North Providence,

Rhode Island 02911
(401) 353-3900

Children's Friend and Service
(statewide voluntary)
2 Richmond Street
Providence,
Rhode Island 02903
(401) 331-2900

Branch Office:

Lakeside Home
150 Lakeshore Drive
Warwick,
Rhode Island 02880
(401) 739-8611

SOUTH CAROLINA

The Children's Bureau of
South Carolina
(statewide public)
Suite 400,
Landmark East Building
3700 Forest Drive
Columbia,
South Carolina 29204
(803) 758-2702

South Carolina State
Department of Social
Services (statewide public)
P. O. Box 1520
Columbia,
South Carolina 29202
(803) 758-3244

SOUTH DAKOTA

Department of Social Services
State Office Building
Illinois Street
Pierre, South Dakota 57501

*Multi-County
Service Area Offices:*

104 South Lincoln
Aberdeen,
South Dakota 57401
(605) 622-2388

627 Fifth Avenue
Brookings,
South Dakota 57006
(605) 692-6301

Courthouse
Chamberlain,
South Dakota 57325
(605) 734-6581

P.O. Box 607
Deadwood,
South Dakota 57732
(605) 578-2405

317 Iowa Street Southeast
P. O. Box 1436
Huron, South Dakota 57350
(605) 352-7337

210 Main Street
Lake Andes,
South Dakota 57356
(605) 487-7607

County Courthouse
Martin,
South Dakota 57551
(605) 685-6526

Main Street
Mission,
South Dakota 57555
(605) 856-4489

P. O. Box 130
116 East 11th Street
Mitchell,
South Dakota 57301
(605) 996-6331

P. O. Box 160
Mobridge,

202

South Dakota 57601
(605) 845-2922

804 North Euclid
Pierre, South Dakota 57501
(605) 224-3521

P. O. Box 279
Pine Ridge,
South Dakota 57770
(605) 867-5861

520 Kansas City Street
Rapid City,
South Dakota 57701
(605) 394-2224

P. O. Box 230
Sisseton,
South Dakota 57262
(605) 698-7673

P. O. Box 1504
405 South Third Avenue
Sioux Falls,
South Dakota 57101
(605) 339-6481

P. O. Box 933
312 Ninth Ave. Southeast
Watertown,
South Dakota 57201
(605) 886-7000

649 West Second Street
Winner,
South Dakota 57580
(605) 842-0400

P. O. Box 219
Yankton,
South Dakota 57078
(605) 665-6241

TENNESSEE

Community Services of
Greater Chattanooga, Inc.

323 High Street
Chattanooga,
Tennessee 37403
(615) 267-2138

Child and Family Services of
Knox County
114 Dameron Avenue
Knoxville, Tennessee 37917
(615) 524-7483

Family and Children's Service
201 23rd Avenue North
Nashville, Tennessee 37203
(615) 327-0833

Tennessee Department of
Human Services
(statewide public)
410 State Office Building
Nashville, Tennessee 37219
(615) 741-3241

TEXAS

Child and Family Service
419 West Sixth Street
Austin, Texas 78701
(512) 478-1648

State Department of Public
Welfare (statewide public)
John H. Reagan Building
Austin, Texas 78701
(512) 475-5777

Hope Cottage-
Children's Bureau, Inc.
P. O. Box 19803
Dallas, Texas 75219
(214) 526-8721

The Edna Gladney Home
(statewide voluntary)
2110 Hemphill
Fort Worth, Texas 76110
(817) 926-3304

The DePelchin Faith Home
100 Sandman Street
Houston, Texas 77007
(713) 861-8136

Harris County Child
Welfare Unit (local public)
4040 Milam St., Suite 301
Houston, Texas 77006
(713) 526-5701

Catholic Family and
Children's Services, Inc.
Archdiocese of San Antonio
(regional voluntary)
2903 West Salinas
P. O. Box 7158
San Antonio, Texas 78207
(512) 433-3256

Family Counseling and
Children's Services
P. O. Box 464
Waco, Texas 76703
(817) 753-1509

Methodist Home
1111 Herring
Waco, Texas 76708
(817) 753-0181

UTAH

Department of Social Services
Division of Family Services
333 South Second East
Salt Lake City, Utah 84111
(801) 533-5031

VERMONT

The Vermont Children's
Aid Society, Inc.
(statewide voluntary)
72 Hungerford Terrace
Burlington, Vermont 05401
(802) 864-9883

District Office:

39 Main Street
Springfield, Vermont 05156
(802) 885-5736

VIRGINIA

Family Service/Travelers Aid
222 19th Street West
Norfolk, Virginia 23517
(804) 622-7017

WASHINGTON

State Department of Social and
Health Services
(statewide public)
Office of Family,
Children and Adult Services
M.S. 410
Olympia, Washington 98504
(206) 753-7002

Children's Home Society of
Washington
(statewide voluntary)
3300 Northeast 65th Street
P. O. Box 15190,
Wedgwood Station
Seattle, Washington 98115
(206) 524-6020

Branch Offices:

117 North Third Street
Yakima, Washington 98901
(509) 457-8139

P. O. Box 8244
Manito Station
(South 4315 Scott Street)
Spokane, Washington 99203
(509) 747-4174

P. O. Box 15190
Wedgwood Station

3300 Northeast 65th Street
Seattle, Washington 98115
(206) 524-6020

405 Denny Building
Walla Walla,
Washington 99362
(509) 529-2130

1105 Broadway, No. 201
Vancouver,
Washington 98660
(206) 695-1325

201 South 34th Street
Tacoma, Washington 98408
(206) 472-3355

WEST VIRGINIA

Children's Home Society of
West Virginia
(statewide voluntary)
1118 Kanawha Blvd. East
P. O. Box 2942
Charleston,
West Virginia 25330
(304) 346-0795

Branch Offices:

203 Monongahela Building
235 High Street
Morgantown,
West Virginia 26505
(304) 296-4796

First Tyler Bank Building
Sistersville,
West Virginia 26175
(304) 657-2800

West Virginia Department of
Welfare (statewide public)
1900 Washington St. East
Charleston,
West Virginia 25305
(304) 348-2400

WISCONSIN

State Department of Health
and Social Services
(statewide public)
1 West Wilson Street
Madison, Wisconsin 53702
(608) 266-3681

Regional Offices:

P. O. Box 228
718 West Clairemont
Eau Claire,
Wisconsin 54701
(715) 835-2174

P. O. Box 3730
1181 Western Avenue
Green Bay,
Wisconsin 54303
(414) 494-9641

3601 Memorial Drive
Madison, Wisconsin 53704
(608) 249-0441

819 North Sixth Street
Milwaukee,
Wisconsin 53203
(414) 224-4501

P. O. Box 697
Schiek Plaza
Rhinelander,
Wisconsin 54501
(715) 362-7800

Catholic Social Services
207 East Michigan Street
Milwaukee,
Wisconsin 53202
(414) 271-2881

District Offices:

430 East Division Street
Fond du Lac,

Wisconsin 54935
(414) 921-2300

1202 60th Street
Kenosha, Wisconsin 53140
(414) 658-2088

129 East Main Street
Port Washington,
Wisconsin 53074
(414) 284-9355

316 Fifth Street
Racine, Wisconsin 53403
(414) 637-8888

630 North Sixth Street
Sheboygan,
Wisconsin 53081
(414) 458-5726

383 West Main Street
Waukesha, Wisconsin 53186
(414) 547-2463

Children's Service Society of
Wisconsin
(statewide voluntary)
610 North Jackson Street
Milwaukee,
Wisconsin 53202
(414) 276-5265

Branch Offices:

307 South Farwell
Eau Claire,
Wisconsin 54701
(715) 835-5915

123 South Webster Street
Green Bay,
Wisconsin 54301
(414) 435-6325

17 South River Street
Suite 256
Janesville,
Wisconsin 53545
(608) 752-0375

1202 60th Street
Suite 110
Kenosha, Wisconsin 53140
(414) 652-5522

2059 Atwood Avenue
Madison, Wisconsin 53704
(608) 249-8506

1111 Maple Street
Neenah, Wisconsin 54956
(414) 725-5432

201 Ceape Avenue
Oshkosh, Wisconsin 54901
(414) 235-1002

818 Sixth Street
Racine, Wisconsin 53403
(414) 633-3591

1121 North Seventh Street
Sheboygan,
Wisconsin 53081
(414) 458-5062

903 Second Street
Wausau, Wisconsin 54401
(715) 842-3343

132 East Grand Avenue
Wisconsin Rapids,
Wisconsin 54494
(715) 421-0480

Jewish Family and
Children's Service
1360 North Prospect Ave.
Milwaukee,
Wisconsin 53202
(414) 273-6515

Wisconsin Lutheran Child and
Family Service
6800 North 76th Street
Milwaukee,
Wisconsin 53223
(414) 353-5000